Steve Robertson

Steve Robertson is best known as part of Scotland The What?, the comedy revue which began at the Edinburgh Festival in 1969 and dropped its final curtain at His Majesty's Theatre, Aberdeen, in 1995.

Steve, Buff Hardie and George Donald were university friends with a passion for comedy and music which began with the Students' Show at Aberdeen University in the Fifties.

Over the years Scotland The What? (described by one critic as "a unique show-business phenomenon") played all the major theatres in Scotland and most of the minor ones, made forays abroad (including to Englandshire) and performed innumerable cabarets and television shows. At their home station, Grampian TV, they occupied prime time every Hogmanay for ten years.

This all culminated in honorary degrees from their Alma Mater, MBEs for services to entertainment in Scotland and, in 2008, the conferral of the Freedom of the City of Aberdeen – a huge honour.

Not so well-known about Steve is that his real, proper job for twenty-five years was as a solicitor. Now he has made a career move into domestic service under the direction of his wife, Eva, with time off – if not for good behaviour – for playing bad golf, watching other sport and doing a spot of gentle glen-walking.

All very appropriate for a retired gentleman who now lives in God's own country of Braemar, Upper Deeside, from which he and Eva venture forth only to visit children and grandchildren, and to do a bit of travelling. And the travelling has not lessened, as Steve finds himself commuting between home and Aberdeen University, by whose students he was delighted to be elected Rector. He is now in his third and final year.

Published in 2010

A catalogue record for this book is available from the British Library

ISBN 978-0-9534534-5-0

Design and typesetting by Leopard magazine
www.leopardmag.co.uk

Printed and bound by
more_ Glasgow

Published by Leopard Press
Auld Logie, Pitcaple, Inverurie, Aberdeenshire AB51 5EE

Scotland
The What?

An Inside Story...
and
Personal Memories

Steve Robertson

Leopard

P R E S S

Dedication

This book is dedicated to the Scotland The What? family, particularly Eva, my wife and typist extraordinary.

Acknowledgments

Maybe there should be more acknowledgements and if so my apologies for any omissions, but I definitely want to thank Buff, Margaret and George for their helpful comments and Gordon Wright, retired Edinburgh publisher, for his interest, his photographs and wonderful spoof letter. And equally warm thanks to Aberdeen Journals for their time and ready co-operation in looking out a multitude of photographs from over the years for me to choose from.

Finally, huge thanks to Lindy Cheyne and Ian Hamilton of Leopard for a professionalism encompassing not only editing, design and technical skills, but also infinite patience and understanding which extend to that extraordinary and wonderful typist mentioned in the Dedication. The four of us really did become a most enjoyable partnership in the venture.

Contents

Foreword

A word of advice to the casual reader who may have noticed that the sub-title to this book is…"An Inside Story". This follows the friendly suggestion of my old friend and retired publisher Gordon Wright who warned, "Put in plenty of anecdotes – people like that".

Always anxious to please therefore   and bearing in mind that you might prefer to regard this book as one to dip into rather than plough through – I would like to point you in the anecdotal direction by mentioning the following chapters all of which are my personal take on events which may well have been seen differently by Buff and George:

1. George unwell; the free taxi-ride; the free lift home.
4. Appearance in drag; visiting the North British; a funeral wake; George, his Mum and Chopin; Buff and a boyhood friend.
5. STW? conceived.
6. Advice from Jimmy Edwards.
9. A visit from James; George's virtuosity.
10. A dreadful dry in Dundee.
11. A bad review; Pavarotti's passport.
12. Flaubert satirised? An Edinburgh flat revisited.
13. Birth of the Pope.
14. Buff's equine allergy.
16. Going full-time.

Anne, Eva, Isabelle and Margaret. Here's to retirement and the boys growing up.

The other bit of help you might like is with the names of the Scotland The What? family – the participants and partners who were:
George Donald and his wife Isabelle (Izzy).
Buff Hardie and his wife Margaret.
James Logan and his wife Anne.
Steve Robertson (your humble author) and his wife Eva.
And our Business Manager Graham Hunter whose wife is Janet.
And our Director from 1993 Alan Franchi and his wife Jane.

Great audience! Thanks for laughing.

Finally the following contractions should be noted throughout:-
STW? – Scotland The What?
HMT – His Majesty's Theatre.
P&J – *The Press and Journal.*
E.E. – *Evening Express*

Introduction

"Starting is easy," said the well-known author whose brains I picked on the subject of attempting this book. "Find a vaguely interesting phrase, preferably in quotations, and you're away."

This seemed good advice and I have taken it. I have started and it was easy. The trouble is – what to do next? Well, the next problem is the qualification offered by my tame author that starting is easy provided you know where to go after the quote. And I do not. Not exactly. Since there were four of us who came to be known as Scotland The What? the story is mixed and multiple with several beginnings and I don't know them all by any means. However, I suppose I know some that are maybe worth telling, but in what order? That's tricky. I don't feel strong enough to decide that right now so instead of starting at the beginning – any of the beginnings – I will start at the end. And this took place on 20th April 2008 when Scotland The What? received the Freedom of their beloved home city of Aberdeen.

Part One

STW? – Endings and Beginnings

1. The Freedom of Aberdeen
20th April 2008

"We got a grand day for it and a'body enjoyed it fine."
– Raymond Leiper, Aberdeen Town Sergeant

That's Aberdeen understatement for you, the economical summary of many hours of sunshine and colour, civic pride and tradition, ceremony and nostalgic reunion, laughter and exhaustion. And the culmination also of a long month and more of worry.

Until early March, preparations for our great day which had been announced nearly a year earlier – ("Don't they know how old we are? We might not be here…" said Buff) – had gone like clockwork and we were most grateful to the new Lord Provost Peter Stephen and his informal sub-committee on behalf of the Council and officials, for consulting closely with us on what they correctly hoped we would like.

Then came the hammer blow from George on the phone from Perth. He had been diagnosed with a malignant tumour and was to undergo surgery urgently, followed by radio and chemo therapy. Our great concern for George descended as an overbearing pall of gloom, not only on his own family, but also on his STW? family and friends. It also meant that George's presence on 20th April was put in doubt.

The man himself would have none of it. "I'll be there," he said bravely.

"The surgeon, in whom I have great confidence, has assured me." But to what extent would he be able to participate?

We had planned a response to the conferral of the Freedom which included, as well as a joint acceptance speech, a new version of the song with which STW? was most closely associated, *Fittie Folk,* where a piano accompaniment was essential. Would George be fit to rehearse, never mind perform to a high standard and then take part in a speech in the most prestigious appearance of his professional life?

The pressure on him was relieved by the knowledge that there was an accompanist in the STW? family who could do that part of the job for him. My wife Eva, a highly accomplished musician, had deputised in emergency before and she immediately began to brush up her pianistic skills lest a contingency plan had to be put in place. Fortunately it was not necessary, but it was a close run thing. Eva's mild disappointment that her practice had been for nought was more than compensated for by the triumph of George not only making it, but being truly inspirational on the day. It was a joy after the ceremony too, when Norman the City photographer was doing lots of official stuff, to see him firmly ensconced in his role of *pater familias*, gamely smiling for the camera from the bosom of his multiplying clan.

But maybe I should go back to the beginning of this great end-day for STW?.

"There's aye a something," of course, even when there is magic in the air and the something on our Freedom day was having to go to HMT and hang around before doing sound checks and receiving a final briefing at a time which was convenient to the staff – very late morning because they had had a late 'get out' from a show the night before.

HMT in the mild chaos of a disorganised morning with the clock ticking, was a bit of a pain. The time for reporting to the Town House for the civic stirrup cup before the procession was 2.45pm and I had only just managed to rush home, get showered and changed before the taxi arrived at 2.25. As I walked towards it I noticed the word 'FREEDOM' on the side and could not help preening myself. How considerate of the management to send a handsome vehicle appropriate for the passenger and the occasion. As I settled into the back seat I gently quizzed the driver. "Nice taxi – interesting to see 'FREEDOM' on the side." "Oh aye," said the driver. "It's for aul' folk and the disabled."

Collapse of proud party whose gas was put to a peep for the rest of the journey. Well, not quite. Conversation was renewed after a diplomatic interval and when the driver had realised the purpose of his fare he dropped me off with the generous acknowledgement, "No charge. This is your day. Enjoy it." What a gent.

And we did. We really did. And the first bit of enjoyment was meeting some of the councillors who were to be processing with us from the Castlegate up Union Street and along Union Terrace to HMT. The assembly point was not the old Town House itself, but the atrium of the Sheriff Court House next door, atrium being a posh description of a space off the main corridor which had lain dead for donkey's years, certainly since when as but a lad (a law apprentice, not a criminal) forty to fifty years before, I was frequently around the courts. In recent times this space had been exhumed by some clever architect and put to agreeable use as a meeting and greeting place. On the odd occasion I have been there it has been a pleasant surprise. Instead of Victorian doom and gloom and echoing stone floors there is Elizabethan space and light and a modicum of carpet comfort – all quite congenial for a bit of socialising and dismantling of preconceptions.

Satire and mickey-taking of municipal authority have been STW?'s stock-in-trade from the very beginning and it was a revealing, not to say humbling experience to get chatting to councillors who were obviously good sorts doing their best, and were big enough to appreciate the joke. There was even one particularly nice gentleman who remembered a number I had done thirty years before and which I had completely forgotten.

But soon it was time to be called to attention for a few photos and to join the 'seventy-six trombones in the big parade'. Not that there was a sign of the Music Man, far less one-hundred-and-ten cornets and rows and rows of tiny piccolos filling the air. Sorry, wrong parade. Naturally and splendidly we had the City Police Pipe Band leading us – us being the Lord Provost at the front in his very grand civic BMW, RGO, then Buff, George and myself in the next car, followed by a good turn-out of local MPs, MSPs, councillors and other civic dignitaries. And the car we had been allocated was not just any car. It was the most gorgeous green goddess, an open tourer Rolls Royce c.1930, specially laid on in replacement of a horse-drawn carriage. (See chapter 14 for the reason we had politely declined this form of transport.)

Since my son, then in Sydney, Australia, is a pal of the car owner's son

A serious point... The Freedom ceremony is traditionally part of a full meeting of the Town Council in formal session. Thank you, Aberdeen.   PHOTO: NORMAN ADAMS–ABERDEEN CITY COUNCIL

and e-mails had been being exchanged between Scotland and Oz, it came as no surprise that the owner was also the driver; retired GP, farmer and classic motor collector Stewart Duncan whom I have known for years. It was an interesting bonus, there being room in the back only for two, to sit in the front beside him. I had not had a catch-up with Stewart for quite a while, so I enjoyed our private chat as we gentled up Union Street in stately fashion, giving the occasional wave to the massed crowds. Well, not quite massed. In fact, only a couple of times meriting the description of a crowd. Very nice people, though, to bother leaving the shops and pubs to give a bit of support which, though not up to what Churchill or Alec Collie got, was very friendly in a puzzled kind of way.

And so to HMT where there really was a most respectable boorachie of folk, outnumbering the largest gathering of photographers we had ever encountered. This was probably the nearest STW? has ever got to knowing what real celebrities (horrible word, but it conveys the atmosphere generated by, with and from a battery of eager clicking cameras) are eager to experience.

There was an element of the surreal about the scene, too. As I made to alight from our Roller the first person who greeted me joyfully was just about the least likely – a smiling, conventional lady, great in years and in everyone's regard – who I thought for a moment could not possibly be

11

Hello folks. A grand day.

who she looked like; then, when I realised that she was indeed who she looked like, caused me to say to myself as I grinned incredulously at her, "Mary Fraser has lost her marbles. Pushing ninety and she's gone nuts!".

Such was the euphoria that permeated that day. Obviously it was very special for us, but by all accounts it was significant for many others too – friends and relatives of each of us, meeting in some cases for the first time in thirty, forty, or even fifty years.

That notion – that STW? had been the catalyst for bringing people together in countless happy reunions – gave me great satisfaction, almost as much as the fact that my own nearest and dearest were there close at hand to offer love and support. Eva was with the other wives, Isabelle and Margaret, in the milling throng outside the theatre, but inside too, I knew, waiting for the ceremony to begin, was our daughter, Sal, son-in-law Steve and our grandchildren Jamie, Finlay, Ellie and Beth all the way from Marlow, Buckinghamshire. And from really far away, from Australia, specially for the occasion, was our son Stephen, bless him. Bless them all.

It is not unusual for Eva and me, in mock Derby and Joan fashion, to croak geriatrically to each other, "Oh, we've been lucky, oh we've been lucky," as we wire in to our Horlicks and digestive biscuits of an early night – but that Freedom day was lucky unlike any other. The experience, no matter how humorously treated, no matter how easily sentimentalised, profoundly touched the heart with its message of the unique personal fortune that had been bestowed upon us.[1] And there is a DVD to prove it all happened – not just the procession, but the ceremony in HMT and the reception and dinner afterwards in the Beach Ballroom featuring a toast by our great friend Jack Webster,[2] and a cabaret, specially written for and much appreciated by us, by The Flying Pigs.

Jack Webster

This most talented group of thirty-somethings have built up a big following over the last five years or so. Seven in number, five men and two girls, there is a resemblance between them and STW? in that their origins lie in the Aberdeen University Students' Show, which means that they do comedy – character-based sketches and monologues with some clever

---

[1] And yet in contrast to our buoyant mood there was unfolding a private story of deep sadness which I feel must be recorded. It was not until the next day that we learned the reason for the sudden disappearance after the meal at the Beach Ballroom reception, of Anne Logan and her family party, which included her sister Laura and brother-in-law Joe. The likelihood, we thought, was that Joe whose health hasn't been too robust in recent years, simply needed an early night – but this was not so. The truth was that Anne's daughter Judith had earlier received on her mobile, and had had the distressing duty of keeping quiet until she judged a suitable break in the proceedings, the appalling news that Laura and Joe's son Stephen had died with dreadful suddenness at the age of forty-six. Amid such public cheer – what personal tragedy.

[2] This is just the first of a number of appearances in the book of the famous author and journalist. Jack has been a supporter not only of STW? but of everything to do with Aberdeen and the North-East of Scotland. Even though he has lived and flourished in Glasgow for more than fifty years he remains a true son of his birthplace, Maud, and has shown his loyalty to his roots in countless ways. For our own part in STW? he gave us most generous coverage in his many newspaper and other articles and outlets over the years and no STW? occasion of any significance was complete without the presence of Jack and, frequently and most welcome, his great friend Ayliff McPhail.

songs thrown in. Another link with The Flying Pigs is that one of their main protagonists – performer, writer and lyricist – is John Hardie, Buff and Margaret's son who, in his father's words, is "nae bad". I rarely disagree with my great friend in matters artistic, but I have to do so here. John is bloody terrific.

There was somehow an inevitability in our day ending strangely. Last to leave as usual, having found ourselves chatting too long to some new-found friend, Eva and I looked for help to get a bus or taxi. "Ye're far ower late for 'at," said an attendant moving at speed towards a door marked 'Staff-Private'. And then, as he disappeared, over his shoulder, "Ye hid plenty warnin' – the last bus left half-an-oor ago an' there's nae taxis either. OK?" Collapse, for the second time that day, of proud party whose gas was now put to an even smaller peep. What the hell to do?

And then, as if by magic, a familiar figure came padding softly up the stairs, greeting us warmly. We had not realised that The Flying Pigs had engaged our old friend David Eastwood to be their back-stage man in charge of sound and lights. And here he was, tail-end Charlie, loading his trusty van – successor to the one which had preceded STW? to many outlandish bits of Scotland where he had been, for us, what we liked to call our 'Sound Wizard'. Rescue was at hand.

We ended STW?'s greatest day bizarrely but appropriately with our old colleague, squeezed the three of us into two front seats with a mountain of technical stuff towering behind us, threatening our very lives as we bumped and shoogled homewards in the small hours through dark and deserted streets.

"Ah well," said David in that quiet Yorkshire way of his. "Not a lot of traffic about. You've certainly got the Freedom of Aberdeen tonight."

2. Going Full-Time
The Biggest Problem

"You'd have to put on your own make-up, you know"
— Eva Robertson

So, after the Lord Provost's Show, back to the beginning…or one of the beginnings. And a very serious one. After doing STW? as a hobby for more than ten years, including latterly a month's run at His Majesty's, Aberdeen, and week-long visits to The King's, Edinburgh and The King's, Glasgow, it was beginning to dawn on us that we might just possibly get round to half-thinking that there was maybe — just a slight chance — of turning the hobby into a full-time job.

This meant heart-to-heart discussions with wives and families — and particularly wives. I don't know what was being said in the homes of my colleagues, but my own dearly beloved brought her own withering insight into the debate. "And finally," she said, "going full-time professional, you'd have to learn to put on your own make-up."

That stopped me in my tracks. We had raked over several reasons why it was not a good idea to go into show business at the age of fifty, but this was the most compelling. Financial security, family responsibilities were one thing, but putting on my own make-up was quite another. Could I cope? Did I want to cope? After all it is difficult to break the habits of a lifetime and I had never put on my own make-up before. Nor had Buff and George; not in thirty years as coarse treaders of the amateur boards anyway. What they got up to in the privacy of their own homes I had no idea, but their marriages seemed to be perfectly sound and, away from the theatre, George's ruddy glow owed everything I was sure to vigorous practice at the piano and a boyhood spent in deepest Aberdeenshire, rather than the merest hint of rouge. As for Buff's interesting pallor, this could only be congenital, dished out at birth along with his asthma by a capricious Mother Nature in meanish mood. Anyway none of us for sure had ever put on our own stage make-up before. Not as schoolboys, not as students, not as members of the old Aberdeen Revue Group, not in thirteen years of STW? so far.

Putting on make-up was not our scene; it was a bit unmanly. It was not a job for lads like us anyway; it was for specialists, gentle-fingered ladies like the delightful and long-suffering Sheila Law who worked wonders on us for years at HMT and to whom we proffered flowers and chocolates in a courtly way before feminism reached Aberdeen. The only non-specialist who got near us was our director James who was far from gentle, but who had to turn his hand to anything when we were doing engagements away from home. He battered the Number Nine on to our cringing faces with such haphazard gusto that it at least took our minds off the opening curtain. Maybe it was James's example – the thought that if he could slap on a bit of make-up so could I – that removed the final barrier. Greasepaint is a metaphor for show business – I thought, "What the hell. Go for it – be a devil. I can do it if I try. Take the plunge".

And I did. For the next umpteen years until our retirement with *The Final Fling* in November 1995 I put myself through the nightly humiliation and scutter of attempting to look a bit healthier than I normally do. What a waste of time. Nowadays, as far as I can see, nobody wears stage make-up. Well not the fellas. Well not most of them. Maybe there is the odd one or two who go in for a bit of fancy scrubbing up, but the tendency towards naturalism and the urge to make a quick exit to the pub as soon as the curtain falls has killed off the daft tradition of artificial enhancement. Pity it had not happened all these years before. It would have saved Eva and me from all that agonising.

This was the beginning, then, of doing STW? full-time as far as I was concerned. The decision made to get serious and subscription paid to Equity, our first engagement in the summer of 1983 was a month's run at the Eden Court Theatre in Inverness.

3. Eden Court Theatre, Inverness
July 1983

"Good afternoon. Found your way all right?"
— Theatrical lodgings proprietor

We had been to the Eden Court several times before and done good enough business for the Director Chris Johnson to keep asking us back – most recently for a solid month during the tourist season. This meant finding accommodation, for which early reconnaissance was required. Eva and I went up to Inverness in early April to look around and had just about drawn a blank on our second day there when our attention was drawn to a guest-house several miles out of town.

More in hope than expectation we set off by highway and secret single-track byway to come finally upon a charmingly battered signpost which whispered *Dunlichity*. It could have been *Brigadoon* – or come straight from the pages of a Scott novel, because there was nothing there except an old kirkyard full of Culloden clansmen. The ghost of Bonnie Prince Charlie may not have been in evidence, but also missing was our destination, Dunlichity Lodge. We discovered it even further off the beaten track, a low pink-harled building tucked away among venerable trees and looking west to a field gate – which didn't lead into a field, but over open moorland and a quarter mile beyond that again, a bonny loch. These were discoveries to be later made, but in the meantime we were greeted at the front door by a tallish, thin man with even thinner hair and a boyish open face — so open that he could scarcely conceal his suspicion of strangers looking for theatrical digs.

"Good afternoon," he declaimed. "Found your way all right?" And the awkwardish body language and wonderfully posh accent suggested either an aristocratic or service background. In fact it was both. Commander Ian A. Scrimgeour Wedderburn R.N.(Retd.) was also a distant scion of the Errol family of that airt near Dundee and he turned out to be an absolute topper of a chap. If he was the naval Commander his equally delightful wife, Desiree (honestly) was the Admiral running the good ship Dunlichity Lodge from her well-ordered kitchen to her equally well-ordered and very gracious dining-room. Ian buttled and scuttled, fetched and carried, walked the dog and ran the car, watched the weather and cricket on telly, lit the fire and polished the brasses and memorably, most memorably, laughed energetically, prematurely and infectiously not *at*, but *before* the end of his own jokes, the while hitching his excitedly Woosterish trousers — which made the stories all the funnier for us. It was as if, enjoying the company of a few kindred spirits, he was rather enjoying being back in the wardroom of his Navy days.

This was all the beginning of a most enjoyable association — for the next ten years or so we stayed with the Wedderburns any time we came to the Eden Court to do the show. And doing the show was really quite boring compared with staying at Dunlichity Lodge. It is quite revealing nevertheless to look at the diary which I kept for that first month of our going full-time professional...

It all started when, bound for Inverness, I went to pick up Buff knowing that he must have had an interesting day or two as he coped with the formalities of retirement from the Health Service after 26 years, the last seven as Secretary of the Grampian Health Board, the most senior administrative post in the organisation. In this official capacity and in the equally serious one of wicket-keeper for Gordonians' Cricket Club, he dismissed the cosy nickname 'Buff' in favour of the cold and conventional 'W.D.Hardie', the initials standing for William Dunbar and, as far as I was concerned, leading to the frequent use of William, not the more hackneyed Buff as a favoured form of address. That explanation is necessary for what follows, as also is the use of brackets inserted now where necessary by way of explanation of people or events in July/August 1983.

And so the diary reads:-

Wednesday 13.7.83. Arrived at William's to find slight domestic shambles – hardly surprising after pressures of previous couple of days including staff presentation and then informal dinner with friends from Scottish Home and Health Department; also presence of house-guest French girl Carole (school exchange?) who is bemused by goings-on. Finally get away and car journey gives essential rehearsal time – of which we do not avail ourselves. Long story instead from William – unusual but very interesting – on events of last day or two. Rendezvous Eden Court 2pm with George, also a bit late (surprise, surprise).[1] Lunch and then run-through of show including very creaky Finale about Loch Ness Monster. Left theatre and technical scutterings of James, Ron[2] and Peter about 5.45 to seek out Dunlichity Lodge again – not difficult though William's normal gloom deepens with the deepening countryside as we reach the back of beyond. Piped aboard by the Commander and his Admiral. Good dinner and a bottle reassure and restore, and enable us to attempt completion of Pope script for Reprise before bed.

Samuel Pepys: "Gadzooks! Steve Robertson's diary is longer than mine."

Thursday 14.7.83. On parade smartish for bacon and egg, then in to Eden Court for Press Call at 11. Friendly interviews and then invited to take off shoes and socks for photos paddling in river. We oblige, though William decidedly unhappy. Barely dry and not yet recovered

---

[1] George's punctuality may have been a bit suspect in relation to events of a social nature, but he was never, ever late for anything important such as "Curtain Up" time – even when put under such severe pressure as having to get himself from Perth Academy to HMT in the days when there was only a single carriageway.

[2] Ron Miller – Technical friend – sound, lights etc. See also Chapter 22. Peter Garland – Stage Manager. See also Chapter 30

from hypothermia we then do chats with Moray Firth Radio and BBC Highland interspersed with records – K. McKellar, H. Gordon and R. Shepherd (the incredible "Up the Dons!"). Late lunch, rehearsal topping and tailing and no time to do much about shaky Loch Ness Monster Finale. Quick shower and sandwich before Curtain-Up, packed house (two for price of one) and very warm reception – even for Nessie – This Is Your Life (indulgent, forgiving, I suspect). Director Chris J. delighted – "Magic," he said. Usual post-show excitement and very hungry but too late for last orders anywhere. Back to Dunlichity having told Commander we won't need supper and he enthusiastically rustles up coffee and sandwiches preceded by comforting G&Ts. Very long exhausting day and can't get through to home on phone.

Friday 15.7.83. Cooked breakfast again after starvation yesterday. Off to theatre, but half-way over moor had to turn back to recover William's lower denture. Post-mortem and further editing of Nessie script. Eva phones – her phone out of order last night. She reports Stephen (our son then nineteen) is driving Margaret Hardie's Mini up to Inverness tomorrow and staying overnight. Nice wee review in *Inverness Courier* and daft paddling pictures in *P&J* and *Daily Record*. Packed house again including establishment dignitaries there to be seen rather than see – therefore a bit teuchie. Dignity and laughter gang nae weel thegither. However, applause at end very warm and reception after show very friendly. Law connections continue with chat with a former secretary at Burnett and Reid (solicitors where I was once assistant) and student contemporary Alistair Beattie, legal king of Caithness and charming wife. Returned HMS Dunlichity for buffet supper. Commander in good form – doesn't like Police who unfairly copped him for speeding downhill – "the buggers".

Saturday 16.7.83. "We're a bit short of spoons actually," said Wedders more in sorrow than apology when one asked for one at brekkers. It is rather odd being served by a senior naval officer, albeit retired. He's a gent anyway. William is joined by his family today to take a log cabin high above Loch Ness and we bring his luggage in to the theatre for transfer on arrival of Margaret and the kids (Katharine and John then aged sixteen and thirteen) or our Stephen, whoever arrives first. Turns out to be Steenie. Drinks, lunch, no sign of Hardie family. Learn later there has been minor disaster – their Maxi thumped and boot badly damaged by another car somewhere west of Elgin. Very satisfactory show in evening – normal, healthy audience and Nessie's health is also slowly improving.

Sunday 17.7.83. Up for breakfast betimes while Stephen sleeps on, catching up after excesses of very late night two days ago and then having to buckle to and drive up in Mini. In to Inverness for Sunday papers. No national reviews – how strange. Back to Dunlichity, sunbathed by loch – warm, warm. Stephen appeared, very hungry after strenuous activity and we go for lunch to local hostelry, Grouse & Trout, which we had heard about. Excellent. Gently back to Dunlichity, then to station with the boy for 4.05pm train. He says he's enjoyed his visit and I believe him. He has a taste for good things in life.

Monday 18.7.83. Light breakfast with George and then wrote letters etc in drawing-room. Lunch at Meallmor Hotel at Daviot – O.K. Back to Dunlichity. Snooze, read papers, bath, afternoon tea with George and then in to theatre early to firm up on one or two things with William who'd had good day with family yesterday. Show O.K. Good audience for a sunny Monday evening. Margaret not too happy with it, however, after seeing it for first time, particularly the Nessie Finale. Quick drink in bar, met Ron Dale who starts in *Show of the North* in Restaurant tomorrow, also Peter Garland's parents. Back to Dunlichity for supper and Commander in fine fettle with stories of aristocratic antecedents and "my own guv'nor – Bunion – that's him hanging on the wall in the Dining-room".

Tuesday 19.7.83. When Jeeves forgot the milk at breakfast I asked for it. Electric response, disappearance to kitchen, quick return, then, "Better sneeze, kid. Brain's a bit dusty today".

Further sort-out of Nessie Finale at theatre – cutting script, re-hanging and re-lighting, fading tape and doing last verse live. Wee drink, lunch and then to Moray Firth Radio for interview with pleasant lad Charlie Stuart, no pretender but quite young.

Very good performance of show in evening – brighter lighting seemed to help pace and audience extremely responsive. Everyone v. cheerful afterwards having quite enjoyed show; also interval delay due to computer cock-up on lighting board. Turned to good effect at beginning of second half – Beechgrove Garden sketch – when audience also enlivened by having time for extra drink. Dickens

Restaurant for supper and catch-up with James and ran William back to log cabin. Coffee with Margaret and thanked her again for catalystic contribution. Late back to HMS Dunlichity and lights out 1.30am.

Wednesday 20.7.83. Not too well slept – lateness plus insomnia – but cheered up at breakfast by the Commander's rendering of a gamey verse about keeping a fire going. In to theatre to finalise Nessie format and rehearse it. Shopping expedition. Lunch at Grouse & Trout. Snooze in heather with papers. Tea with George. To theatre where slightly larger but teuchier audience than last night. Couple of missed lighting cues, but Nessie went like clockwork – much happier with it now. Drink afterwards while Show of the North going on – enjoyable. Chris J. invited us back 1985. Return to HMS Dunlichity for supper and earlyish hammock.

Thursday 21.7.83. Glorious morning. Sat under tree after breakfast. Got up. Walked about. Listened to birds. Looked at the sky. Wondered what to do – oh decisions, decisions! In to town to tackle shopping again. Bought lots. Booked Alan and Olga (visiting in-laws) into Glen Mohr Hotel. Pie and Pint lunch. Back to Dunlichity. Tea on lawn with George. Ablutions. Reported for duty Eden Court. How many idiots could possibly want to come to theatre on such a lovely evening? Several hundred, it transpires – many of whom are, however, having a quiet doze. Hard work. Drink with Jim Love – knowledgeable journalist and good guy, thanked him for Courier notice. Back Dunlichity for supper.

Friday 22.7.83. Brilliant sunshine again. Telephone activity re interest in Rhynie croft by old friends and clients. Visit to wee loch – sunbathing, dipping, exploring margins – bliss is it, etc. – and even to be middle-aged is very heaven in this corner of the world. Grouse & Trout for beer and sandwich. Jolly wedding in progress – marquee on lawn and bubbly abounding among morning suits, kilts and flowery hats. Pottered in car – Loch Ashy, Torness, Loch Duntelchaig. Back in time for afternoon tea on lawn with George who'd been bird-watching. Commander as officer of the watch intimates temperature of eighty-two degrees in shade at 4pm. Phone-call from Ian Robertson (solicitor Stonehaven, no relation, nice guy) accepting croft offer – verbal bargain. Client delighted. In to theatre where thin house includes Commander and Mrs Wedderburn – pity – and also Buff's friends Robin and Sara Stewart (Robin S. Buff's opposite number in Highland Board, NHS) Consoling drink and back to HMS Dunlichity for supper and amused and amazing critique. Funny personal reminiscences – Desiree had been at Kingseat (in 1983 a hospital) as a WREN during War.

Saturday 23.7.83. Heat haze and bleating sheep from farm enclosure just across the bank. In to Eden Court, via purchase of tapes and getting parking ticket, for big rendezvous. I win £1 bet with George when Isabelle and Claire (younger daughter) arrive before Eva. Late but great! Everyone drifts off – Margaret and kids homeward, George and Izzie to shop for 80th birthday (whose?). To Dunlichity. Guided recce of environs for Eva – especially loch where Commander and Brora (black lab) are disporting themselves. Girls decide to stay aboard while we go to work. Bigger audience and also very appreciative. Back immediately for delightful supper. Commander in great form as he suggests ways of improving show – including His Holiness kissing ground and Pipe-Major marching on spot.

Sunday 24.7.83. Muster parade for late breakfast. Quick thought on lawn – lovely, hazy sunshine again – about suitable remarks at Forres Gala where we've been invited. Departure in convoy and arrive Heather Hotel, Forres, to meet two Round Table chaps, Archie and Tony, and have lunch also with Mr and Mrs George Barron (of Beechgrove Garden). Procession to Park led by Pipe Band, William and I in vintage Lea Francis, our George in Morris Cowley two-seater, George Barron in unidentified jalopy and he opens proceedings. Then we say a few words and judge Fancy Dress Competition before "mingling". Surprise meeting with Bob and Hilary Gloyer and Moira and Johnny Dickson (old University friends). Part company after an hour, George and Izzie for Banchory and 80th birthday party (George's Dad), Buff to Aberdeen in battered Maxi and I back to have walk in sunshine with Eva. Quiet dinner, a little telly, Sunday papers and so to bed.

Monday 25.7.83. First through to breakfast – Donalds very late returning last night after birthday trip (lost at Culloden – so did Prince Charlie). Eva and I go to golf at Culcabock and she wins 3 and 2. Rain in air but doesn't come to much. Wish it would pour and drive folk in to theatre. Back to Dunlichity to meet our groupies for tea – Izzy and Claire, Alan and Olga who arrive with Sal (our daughter, then nearly twenty-one). Cheery claque to whom we're grateful for presence in what James calls a "quality" house – i.e. pretty thin.

Tuesday 26.7.83. Yet another drouthy day. Big turn-out for breakfast prompts recurring catch-phrase from Commander, "More bread?" We meet Olga and Alan for coffee at Glen Mhor. Fond farewells and sight-seeing – Culloden, Cawdor – human scale with funny captions. Back for tea on lawn. To theatre and another quality house. Philosophical return to bosoms of families and comforts of the table.

Wednesday 27.7.83. Less warm and Ancient Mariner of Dunlichity reports temperature of sixty-eight point two degrees. Pow-wow at theatre with James re forthcoming Perth and Edinburgh engagements. Lunch with girls at Grouse & Trout which they like very much. Eva, Sal and I go for swim in loch. Marvellous. Eva takes Sal to station for 5.48 train. To theatre for yet another quality house. Gey teuchie, but better than thirty only at Show of the North downstairs. Revolutionary transposition of Edinburgh Castle and Bruce and the Spider calculated to transform first half amazingly does not. Back to Dunlichity where James our guest. I over-indulge.

Thursday 28.7.83. Cooler and cloudy. Donalds go on Whisky Trail to Tomatin to visit relative. William and I to theatre for further confab with James. Lunch Kingsmills Hotel with Farquharsons and Ashers (very good friends from Inverness and Nairn) who are in great form with stories of US and The Masters at Augusta. Very good house in evening – surprising 'cause still good weather and rival attraction over the wall in Northern Meeting Ground in shape of Tattoo. Show goes like clockwork – nary line or laugh missed and smashing audience. Back to HMS Dunlichity for very cheery supper slightly dampened by reports of two prangs – George in ditch due to speed of on-coming car and Margaret in Aberdeen – Carden Place when hired car dunted from behind, like Maxi!

Friday 29.7.83. Gale-force winds, high clouds and sunshine. A day for golf? Yes – out of town to Rosemarkie. We met by chance long-lost cousin of Eva's and her husband – Margaret and Forbes from Liverpool. Enjoyable golf despite impossible wind and Eva wins again. She's a killer. Drops me off at theatre for shower and snooze in dressing-room and Graham (Hunter, our Business Manager) wakes me up – just arrived from Aberdeen for week-end. Friday audience a bit stiff again but we survive and are then entertained to drinks by

Faculty of Solicitors for Ross and Sutherland – very pleasant. Back to HMS Dunlichity for a fine supper of fish and chips and summer pudding.

Saturday 30.7.83. More and more on waking I look at weather and possible effect on size of evening's audience. Just a hint of rain today, hopefully? Hearty breakfast for most of house-party, particularly appreciated by Graham – off leash. Everyone goes off to do own thing – Eva and I car run exploring – Errogie, Loch Mhor, Garthlock, Falls of Foyers, Dores pub after bonny walk. Back to Dunlichity for tea and snooze before rigours of evening. Interrupted by phone-call from daft client about title to her lock-up. To theatre for big house and excellent response – despite rain staying away. Drink afterwards with friends of George, Sandy and Audrey Christie. Back to HMS Dunlichity for splendid nosh and bun-fight with the Commander on form recollecting Will Hay, Moore Marriot and Graham Moffat.

Sunday 31.7.83. Dreams are subject of breakfast conversation. Last night I bumped into Lord Olivier in the Amatola Hotel, Aberdeen (a block of flats these many years). He was stoned – dead worried at thought of standing in for Keith Michel in Amadeus at HMT. Everyone has different arrangements for our day off. Eva and I have walk round loch then join George and Isabelle for drinks at Meldrums (friends and neighbours of Wedderburns) at Clachan. Delightful secluded spot and delightful open people. Picnic lunch, snooze and Sunday papers in heather. Dinner at Grouse & Trout with our hosts as guests – they've been very good to us. Isabelle and Claire leave for Perth, but Margaret has arrived again for a few days' peace and quiet as a result of which there are complicated bedroom flittings. Commander in his organisational element. "Mr Hardie will close the loop" – whatever that means.

Monday 1.8.83. Margaret has dreamt that William has acquired tartan shorts of outsize dimensions. Are we that desperate for audience laughter? Hearty breakfasts all round and then William and I retire to Drawing Room to consider response to Evening Express proposal for new weekly column. Graphics they've sent nae great and we'll have to tell them. In to town for golf – course too busy so we enjoy sunshine and sandwiches then explore Ness Islands before Eva leaves for home – very reluctant after nine perfect days. Very satisfactory audience for show and performances also up to scratch despite hyena laugh somewhere and a few corpses from us. An extra line creeps in to "Under the Carpet" – "An expert on foosty newspapers? Div ye get folk like 'at?" After show Ann and Gordon Farquharson come to HMS Dunlichity for supper and enjoy spectacle of STW? under naval discipline.

Tuesday 2.8.83. George says he's had a nightmare – playing a piano concerto with the SNO and could not see the conductor for a big tree growing out of the platform. After breakfast William and I repair to Drawing Room to work on E.E. column "Ernie and Flo" (later changed to "Dod and Bunty", written in tandem for first few months and then by Buff solo for next twenty years). We speak to Ranald Allan. features man of E.E., and he seems happy with what we are doing. Then we turn attention to "The Italians" (see Chapter 21) Episode 2 which we began in Glasgow seven weeks ago. Sort out tricky plot ready to attack afresh another day. Lunch at Grouse & Trout and more exploration of byways – view from above Errogie on wee road from Torness particularly fine. Return via Inverfarigaig, Dores and Loch Duntilchaig. Tea and briefing from Commander on eradication of moles including use of smoke bombs and esoteric plant with malodorous roots (caper or mole spurge?) To theatre and show generally goes well with a couple of changes in "Spy" sketch.

Wednesday 3.8.83. Wakened early without need for usual knock from Commander. Hearty breakfast needed for golf at Nairn with Jimmy Asher and Gordon Farquharson – very good players – too good for me, but very enjoyable and I did have some holes which weren't too bad. Lunch at Ashers and Jimmy leaves early to attend Nairn Show – sartorially splendid in bunnet, cycle clips and Augusta tie. Return to meet lads at theatre for pore-over on Edinburgh and Perth. Very good house and drinks afterwards with high-heid-yins of Scottish Opera. Back to flagship for celebratory supper – Hardies' twentieth anniversary. Charming card from Commander and Admiral and we pretend house white is bubbly.

Thursday 4.8.83. Busy day ahead so hearty breakfast again. To town to open Flower Festival at Cathedral next door to theatre. An enormous and jovial Provost and a small, worried Precentor (Little and Large) welcome us and a very solemn, serious lady gives us the guided tour. From sacred concerns we proceed to the secular – we are guests of the Black Isle Show – just George and I, William having begged off in favour of ploy with Margaret. Welcomed to official double-decker Portakabin with warm gins and tonic, then marquee lunch seated between Lord and Lady (Hamish) Gray (ex-MP) – charming – and opposite Admiral Sir John Hayes and Charles Kennedy (new young MP). Invited to say a few words on mikes to big crowd who rightly weren't interested and we made no impact whatsoever. Back to Dunlichity to recover and say farewell to Margaret homeward bound on evening train. Good house for evening show but response suggested they'd come for a sleep after Black Isle Show. My own sleep not too good since sharing room with William for last couple of nights. Commander claimed he had "closed the loop" but I wished William had closed his mouth.

Friday 5.8.83. Fractured sleep. To town by Bunachtan to enjoy view – time running out – meeting with James and near finalisation of Perth show. Drink in bar and chance meeting with old university friend Ivor Sutherland, Director of Education somewhere. To Kingsmill Hotel to book accommodation for Mum and Dad who visit next week, then to Golf Clubhouse for beer and sandwich and bump into Ron Dale of Show of North. Nice guy and we arrange a game. Back to Dunlichity to rest up for evening which proves very good – response as well as size of house. William claims there was even a laugh in Edinburgh Castle. Drinks afterwards with Moira and Johnny Dickson (old university friends). Phone-call home, Eva a little worried and tells me of death of Roy Milne. I feel very sad and somehow a little guilty. Much chat about him over supper with William and George. Gloom dispelled by Commander acting as ship's jester with funny stories which he gets wrong and are all the better for it. It's the way he tells 'em.

Saturday 6.8.83. Lovely day again. Packing, purchase of mementos, payment of account, farewells taken including to Guv'nor Bunion – old chap on the wall. Transfer to home of Robin and Sara Stewart, Beech Hill, Crown Avenue, Inverness. Very pleasant. Light lunch Kingsmills Hotel – except George who says he is fasting. William compensates with trifle. Afternoon spent lazing – inside at telly and outside in garden. William retreats topless to quiet corner to slave over a couple of lyrics – Rentokil and My Way. Evening great house and response after slowish first half. Afterwards nice visits from two other Dunlichity residents and Colin and Joy Jackson (former member of Aberdeen Revue Group – now sadly deceased). Cheery supper at Dickens – James, Anne, William, George and I.

Sunday 7.8.83. Long lie 'cos no ship's bell/Skipper's knock… discipline sloppy in new quarters. Phone home to wish Stephen Happy nineteenth Birthday – he sounds perky, as does Sal, Eva slightly less so – pressure of kids at home? Working with William – on Perth programme and then "The Italians". No lunch but many chocolate biscuits for afternoon tea – William's selection. We go to Kingsmills for dinner and I phone home again later to learn birthday barbeque with grandparents has gone well and Eva much happier. Reassured. And so to bed with plethora of Sunday papers and trannie-dipping.

Monday 8.8.83. A sumptuous summer's day again – but William and I brave ourselves to renew attack on "The Italians" and, when breaking for lunch, decide to go out of town. We fetch up at Evanton – Foulis Ferry? – and have Italian nosh before continuing to work *al fresco* overlooking sparkling Cromarty Firth. Brain cudgelling accompanied by guitar strumming from long-haired, dark-moustached lad lamenting – what? The loss of his shirt maybe? Back to town and watched a bit of telly – Athletics from Helsinki where Wells sunk but not without trace or honour. Very good house and reception for a steamy Monday and we have drinks afterwards with Ashers and Farquharsons. Late night Indian at Rajah International where Hurricane Giulianotti (character referred to by Pope in show) had his mince and tatties vindaloo.

Tuesday 9.8.83. To Aberdeen by train to attend funeral of Roy Milne (see Chapter Seventeen, Item 5). I find myself beside young mother and infant and cower in terror behind newspaper at wet and windy noises. The baby is quite noisy too. Sal meets me off train in Dad's car – Eva at golf – and takes me home to change. Pleased to see very good turnout of legal profession. Seated beside Ian Edward (very close and old friend who succeeded Roy in firm of C&PH Chalmers in 1964). Inadequate minister redeemed by eloquent tribute from Alan Frazer (Roy's old university friend and writing partner in Students' Shows of the thirties who did rather better professionally). Attended lunch at RNU Club on kind invitation of Frank Connon (senior partner of Campbell Connon, Solicitors, where Roy was backroom special assistant) and appreciated company of soul-mates of Roy's, people on side of angels I am glad to meet including Roy's daughter Susan and husband, also Phil Love, Jock Hendry (partners in Campbell Connon – Jock still there, Phil retired Principal, Liverpool University), George Runcie (ex BBC Scotland) who once interviewed me for a job at Roy's request – very friendly – and others too many to mention. Time for one course only before dashing, but cliché holds that Roy "would have enjoyed the occasion" – one of respect, compassion, humour, affection. Sal spirits me to train mowing down pedestrians en route. Very hot in train – dozed. On return William produced afternoon tea and éclairs from M&S. Very good house again and afterwards we have supper in bar downstairs and are joined by our colleagues from Show of the North who are a very pleasant lot – unassuming, no-side folk one of whom, Billy Anderson, is also very funny with true showbiz stories. Very late back to bed, very tired. Some day.

Wednesday 10.8.83. To Eden Court for rehearsal of Perth show and Rentokil Van (new item, lyric and music by Hardie and Donald) should be useful addition to repertoire. Lunch restaurant, chat with Chris Johnson. Back to Crown Avenue to watch Athletics on telly – terrific stuff – then edge forward with "The Italians" helped by cup of tea in the garden. Evening's performance, house and response, all of first order – probably best of season. Visit back-stage from David and Irene Anderson on holiday (old University friends who have bobbed up over the years). To Dickens for delicious Chinese supper. And so to bed all in good form.

Thursday 11.8.83. Cooler but pleasant day for golf and a game with Ron Dale of Show of the North at Culcabok. High stakes of 50p for first nine, 50p for second nine and 50p for eighteen plus showbiz gossip almost put me off my stot, but receiving eleven strokes I triumph by one hole. Most enjoyable. Grouse & Trout for solo lunch, encountering crashed car en route – three youngsters distraught but O.K. and I phone police from Inverarnie. Mid-afternoon to Kingsmills Hotel to meet Mum and Dad who are in excellent form. Show in evening very good, though slightly marred in first half by minor aberrations – a wee dwam from William and a frog in the throat from myself in "The Spider". Dinner at Dickens with Mum and Dad. Late to bed after further chat with Good Companions.

Friday 12.8.83. To Kingsmills a.m. to set folks on right road to
Dundonnel – not entirely plain sailing as I try to guide them on to
Kessock Bridge, since Dad insists on following me round and round
the roundabout just before it. Golf solo and score 95 without
cheating – much. Back to billet for modest lunch – tray in front of
telly. Peace broken by return of Hardie carful from various ploys,
George from Dingwall where he'd gone to meet friends and
Graham from Aberdeen train. Last night of show rather good indeed.
Everything gets just about maximum – despite the odd practical joke
from stage staff. Champers with theatre governors after show, then
supper in restaurant. Farewells to our friends in Show of the North,
then back to billet. Coffee and multiple drams. And so to bed.

4. Edinburgh Festival Fringe
1969 and 1970

"Good morning ladies, and welcome..."
— Myself to assembled company

An earlier beginning took place on 8th September 1969, on which subject I have been asked to give a talk a number of times, so from the notes I prepared at the time I am able to reproduce fairly accurately what I said. The caveat is that there is a fair bit of exaggeration here and there. Not only exaggeration. The truth may also have been bent a little on the basis that it is a mistake – particularly when you're trying to engage an audience – to spoil a good story with complete veracity.

Anyway, here is my talk to an audience of Probus Ladies.

"Good morning, ladies, and thank you, Madam Chairman, for your kind introduction. It's very nice to be here – in fact, looking around I probably speak for quite a few when I say it's very nice to be anywhere at our age. However, speaking entirely personally, I do appreciate the warm welcome – it is reassuring to be applauded in when you know you are well on the way to being clapped oot... which is, I must admit, an old STW? joke – intentionally so, because, having been given free rein to speak about anything I liked, it wasn't a difficult decision for me to be very self-indulgent and to offer you some personal memories of STW?, a subject close to my heart, if only for the fact that it's probably the only thing I know more about than anyone else – apart from my old friends, George Donald and Buff Hardie. And they're not here to answer back … and I must not forget our late and much-lamented Director, James Logan, who may, however, who knows, be listening in from a wee cloud up there somewhere and waiting to give me critical notes on this performance – waiting sometime in the future – in what I do hope is the not-too-near future!

Anyway, as I say, it's a big thrill to be here – my biggest thrill since being invited to Balmoral to do a show for the Queen – and Prince Albert. And that, of course, is another old joke from STW? It would have been part of what we called our 'Opening Chat' – the bit of the show at the start when we would supposedly – in our dreams – drift on elegantly – or, more accurately at the end of our careers – hirple on – hirple, hobble, shamble, totter on to the stage – there to engage in, also in our dreams, a bit of sparkling repartee, witty badinage, light-hearted banter effortlessly articulated – but in reality I can tell you laboriously conceived – because even one decent *ad lib* could take a brain-cudgelling couple of hours, if not days.

I am sure some of you will know that the blank sheet of paper is a fearsome sight – and never more so, we found, than when we had an Opening Chat to write, because it's not nearly so easy trying to be amusing as yourself as it is being a character in a sketch.

Some of the Opening Chats were pretty turgid, but I do remember one of the better sequences which went like this: 'Ochone, ochone – hoorichan horrichan – hamei geerie plate brochan tine haske'. Now that may not be very funny, but these days you get a £20,000 grant just for saying it. We picked up that bit of the Gaelic on a recent visit to Inverness – we were up there doing a rather saucy little cabaret for that most happy-go-lucky lot, the Synod of the Free Presbyterian Kirk. It wasn't a great weekend – I got a parking ticket – which was most unlucky – that was the first crime the Highland Police had solved since the Massacre of Glencoe. When we were there we did learn, however, that the Loch Ness Monster was born two million years ago – just about the length of time in Aberdeen where we've been waiting for the Western Peripheral Road…".

Note the topical comment at the end which could be useful anywhere we went, changing the reference, of course, to whatever project had been awaited for a very long time.

Now if this talk were a show – an evening with STW? instead of a delightful coffee morning with you ladies – what you would have been hearing so far might be described as the Opening Chat – the hope being to break the ice, relax the audience and get them on your side – the same idea today. But today, instead of going from the Opening Chat into a sketch or a song – which you might prefer – I am going to continue with my bit of self-indulgence and I am going to tell you a little about the history of STW? which began officially on 8th September 1969 when we opened on the Edinburgh Festival Fringe in St Mary's Roman Catholic Cathedral Hall, Albany Street, just round the corner from Leith Walk, Edinburgh.

As I say, that was the official beginning, but unofficially, long before any of us knew each other, it began twenty years or so earlier, not at University where we met and got involved in the annual Students' Show, that great North-East fund-raising institution which happily carries on to this very day, but actually at school. Picture the scene:

Buff Hardie, fifth year schoolboy, was in the Robert Gordon's College play 'Surrexit Christus', a serious religious work, and I, a third year schoolboy, was in the Aberdeen Grammar School play 'The Moon is Down' by John Steinbeck, also a piece of serious drama. Rival schools, rival productions less than a mile apart, both playing to packed houses and, looking back bitterly, neither Buff nor I got the tiniest percentage of the box-office takings. In Surrexit Christus Buff played the part of Pontius Pilate's wife – a beautiful lady – so this was not type-casting – and in The Moon is Down I played a Norwegian housewife of doubtful virtue.

This was the only time either of us ever appeared in drag and the experience was so traumatic that we never did it again. The nearest I ever got was in a sketch called *Bruce and the Spider* and I was the Spider – and the only way you can play a Spider, in contrast to the testosterone-charged Warrior King Robert the Buff Hardie Bruce, was to make the Spider as jessie as possible and as camp as a row of tents.

Anyway – back to school days and Buff as Pontius Pilate's gorgeous beloved. I am told that he wore a white sheet which he had pinched from his mother's clothes-line and which was draped fetchingly over one rather pimply adolescent shoulder leaving the other one looking even more pimply and adolescent. Meanwhile, as the Norwegian *femme fatale* I had on my Mum's high heels and my auntie's wig, among other embellishments of style and sophistication.

Knowledgeable critics and kind friends have said that Buff and I were never as funny again. I was a late developer – as you will probably have gathered today – and I must have been quite a bonny loon before the callowness of youth set in; but Buff was never bonny. At seventeen he looked sixty-seven, so it is only within the last few years that he has grown into his real age.

The point of this narrative, however, is that while I shared one schoolboy stage with a cast which included a lad of brilliant thespian potential, Ian Cuthbertson (who sadly died recently), Buff shared that other schoolboy stage with a boy from Maud called Jack Webster. Now Jack was also a late developer – so late that Robert Gordon's College to its shame failed to spot his abilities and his parents were told he had no future there. So that was it for Jack – cast out, denied the chance even to sit his Highers, shattered and disillusioned, troubled by dodgy health and a bad stammer, he had to make his own admirably resilient way in journalism which, as we all know, turned out wonderfully well. By 1969 Jack was a successful features writer in Glasgow with the *Scottish Daily Express* in its glory days. So that year, twenty years after leaving Gordon's – when Jack spotted that there was this little group from Aberdeen coming to the Fringe with a show called STW? and he saw that Buff Hardie – his old acquaintance in the Gordon's College Dramatic Club – was involved, he suggested to the newspaper's theatre critic Neville Garden that he might go along and see what this show was all about. Well, Neville did come along and he must have liked what he saw, because he gave us a very favourable review – the very first review STW? ever had – which sported the headline *Funniest Show In The Festival,* as a result of which that week in Edinburgh turned out to be a great success.

I remember little or nothing about actually performing the show, but a lot of the surrounding details remain strong in my mind – such as the fact that Buff and I had nowhere to stay. George came through every night from Perth where he was living, and went home after the show because he had to teach next day, but Buff and I kipped down in sleeping bags on the bare scruffy lino in a rather dank, miserable dressing-room in the basement of the hall, overlooked by bleak pictures of the Virgin Mary who looked even less happy down there in the dungeons than we were. Also down in the dungeon with us was our newly appointed Business Manager Graham

Hunter (well known lawyer in town – very respectable and conservative with a small 'c') and this was his first introduction to the glamour of show business – and a severe test of friendship which we all happily survived. Graham has remained with STW? right up to the present day when he still has a bank account for us for the trickle of pennies which come in from a couple of CDs we have put together over the last four or five years in our retirement.

But back to the dungeon…After a couple of sleepless nights – so rendered by the spooky pictures and the sound of the screaming cisterns from the urinals next door, punctuated by Hardie and Hunter's heavy snoring – yes, after this torture I decided, like Lazarus, to take up my bed – or rather my sleeping-bag – and walk – straight upstairs to the hall, the auditorium and on to the stage, where at least there was a nice clean and really quite comfy carpet. I seem to remember it was a blue Axminster with a flowery pattern which Graham had cadged from a Discount Warehouse in down-town Leith – and I slept quite well there all alone in front of a full house of empty seats – seats which creaked occasionally (they were definitely creaking, not laughing.) That was all after the show – very late.

Before the show, ablutions were a problem. There were no showers in this squalid, sanctimonious basement and I remembered a dodge from National Service days. I went to the nearest big anonymous hotel which was the North British, long before it became the Balmoral, where it was not too difficult to mingle with the crowds coming and going, then slip upstairs to find a bathroom or shower-room. This was before the days of *en suite* facilities to which access would have been impossible. The hygienic arrangements on every floor were cavernous echoing chambers of Victorian splendour and what appeared to be medieval sanitary ware, for the comfort and convenience only of the hotel's paying guests. But I wisna payin'. Although I did have a pang of conscience, I consoled myself with the thought that if this was swicking a wee bit in an ungodly sort of way, at least cleanliness was next to godliness. And at the end of the week when my wife Eva came down for the final performance we checked in officially and salved my well-brought-up Scottish conscience.

All went well, until one evening when I was getting out of the shower I was aware of voices outside the door. There were angry mutterings and I thought I detected an American accent. "Somebody's been in there a long time"…a female voice. Complaining. And another female voice agreeing. My God! It dawned on me that I had unwittingly wandered into a ladies-only shower-room. And no escape, except by the door I had come in. I was terrified. I got dressed as quickly as I could, mind racing, took a deep breath and opened the door. There was a queue of wifies in dressing-gowns with towels and toilet bags. The American at the front said, "My God – it is a man!" And as I swept past with as much dignity as I could muster, I said, "I wouldn't go in there, ladies. There's something very funny about that shower-room – I went in a woman and I have come out a fella." Then I ran like hell.

Well, that was more than forty years ago and we lasted for the next twenty-six years – until the end of 1995 after a final season at HMT and a Hogmanay show on Grampian Television. HMT was our favourite venue not just because it was at home, but because it was definitely the best theatre we ever played – the most beautiful, the most welcoming, the most cared for. Excellence, of course, begins at the top and the boss was Jimmy Donald who, as skipper, ran the tightest of ships, ably supported by his younger brother, Peter, and his Technical Director, Edi Swan, a great pal from away back in our Students' Show days. Jimmy took us to H.M.T. first of all in 1971 after our second visit to the Fringe – this was for two nights and we did three – the third being a Sunday which was unheard of in those days and we went back every couple of years – '71, '73, '75, '77, '79 – for four weeks in the summer. After this there was a three-year break while the theatre was being renovated, at the end of which we were in process of going full-time. We did six weeks at Christmas '82, and then summer seasons in '84, '86, '88 and '90, then autumn seasons in '93 and '95.[1]

So HMT was high in our affections, not only for artistic reasons, but also for the practicality of keeping the financial boat afloat. Which was very important because when we went full-time in '82/'83 a number of people in their kindly, tactful, Aberdonian way said we were barking mad leaving, as we were, the security of conventional careers which were reasonably well remunerated.

I encountered the same sort of attitude back in 1969 when I was fixing up that Edinburgh venue I mentioned – St Mary's Cathedral Hall. As you maybe know, I was a solicitor and I remember getting in touch with my law firm's Edinburgh correspondents – rather stuffy, very correct. I said to

---

[1] Long seasons meant having to help with publicity which meant having to get photographed doing daft things. See photo opposite.

How did we let ourselves in for this?

PHOTO: ABERDEEN JOURNALS

my opposite number there, "Hello Bill – Steve Robertson, Aberdeen, here".

"Oh hello Stephen. How's the frozen north today? Managing to keep the sheep out of Union Street?"

"Bill – I'm phoning on behalf of people looking for a suitable hall for doing a show on the Fringe…"

"Oh dear, not really my line of country – you get some fearful scruff coming to the Fringe. Who are these people? I wouldn't have thought you would take on that sort of client."

"Oh well, there are exceptions…"

"Yes I suppose so …the main question is, do they have the funds to pay the rent? Are they clean enough and tidy? They're not into drugs, are they?"

"I think they should be OK. I can vouch for them personally."

"You can? Well who are they then?"

"Well as a matter of fact…they are …a couple of friends and myself…"

"Dear God…don't tell me you're a performer of some sort? You don't sound like one of these people to me…Have you told your senior partner?"

"I am the senior partner…"

"Dear God…so you are…I'd quite forgotten…amazing! The totally unintended but for yourself, fortuitous consequence of death and retirement – lucky sod that you are…"

"So, Bill, you think you might be able to help?"

"Oh Stephen – don't be daft – what about your professional reputation? Your clients will find out."

"No, no, Bill – I'm just taking a week's holiday – instead of going off with friends to play golf or go fishing, we'd like to go to the Fringe."

"Oh well – I still think you're mad, but I'll see what I can do…"

And he came up trumps…and that's how we came to be brooded over by the Virgin Mary and other gloomy icons in the dreary dungeon. Bill and I became good friends as well as professional colleagues – and a few years later I used to send him a couple of tickets every time we went to the King's in Edinburgh. Now long retired, he came up specially from Edinburgh to attend our Freedom Ceremony.

Looking back I suppose it was quite difficult in those early years to reconcile the job with the hobby – different culture in those days – particularly as the hobby began to earn a bit more than beer money and to impinge on time and energy and not just professional, but family commitments.

I think it was in the mid-seventies that the funeral of a client, a very old lady, took place the same day we were opening at HMT. Funeral 3pm. Curtain up 7.30pm.

After the Crematorium, quickly back to the office at the request of the eldest son to get the will and return to the deceased lady's home – the old family home where everyone had gathered, some from afar, including the eldest son, the main Executor, from Glasgow. When I got there after four o'clock the place was already hotching – heaving with smoke and drink and jollification – a real copper-bottomed, genuine wake. I declined pressing invitations to refreshments and tried to get through the formalities of reading the Will as expeditiously and solemnly as I could against a background of alcohol-induced interruptions. Phrases came wafting through the atmosphere...

"Oh, I wis wintin' the grandfather clock..."

"I'm nae interested in the sycamore bedroom suite..."

"I wonder fit happened tae yon canteen o' cutlery in the glory hole?"

And so on. A time of characteristic family concern and endearments...

Anyway, I got through it, dealt with questions and was anxious to leave, since it was now well after six. Then one of the younger sons, a local chap who happened to be a personal client, said, "Aye, you'll be keen tae get awa, Mr Robertson. I see you've got yer show in the theatre this wik..." Puzzled looks all round. A pause and then the eldest son from Glasgow said "What show's this?"

At which point it was explained to him that this was a comedy show – sketches, songs and so on, which, as I cringed with embarrassment, all sounded so cheap and trivial. Anyway, after the explanation the eldest son who had listened most carefully delivered the withering line, "Well, Mr Robertson, I'm sure I speak for all the family when I say that we're greatly comforted to know that the solicitor with the responsibility of winding up our dear departed mother's estate is a bloody comedian..."

And then there was another time a very nice elderly farming couple came into the office one Friday – after the Mart and the shopping. And the lady said, "Oh, Mr Robertson – we were in tae the theatre tae yer show last week and it wis affa good – you know, Mr Robertson, I think you're in the wrang job". This was kindly meant, but fairly gave her husband an opening. Aul' Jimmy glowered up frae aneath his bonnet and

Andy Stewart - Halls of Fame cast 1984. Andy did not sing *Scottish Soldier* **and I did not sing** *Scottish Plumber.*

said, "God, Mary – you never spoke a truer word. That's the first sensible thing I have heard you say this year".

Such were the discouragements of performing. And they didn't just happen to me. George tells the story from his boyhood days in Huntly when he was showing promise at the piano and was very keen; but his Dad wasn't, and he would say to him as he gave him a clip on the lug – "Would ye stop playin' that damned piano, George – I canna get my paper read".

His Mother's influence was quite telling as well. The wee lad went to the pictures with her on one occasion – the Huntly Odeon. The film showing was *A Song to Remember,* about the life of Chopin starring Cornell Wilde as Chopin and Meryl Oberon as his lover Georges Sand. And there was a famous scene when the great man, stricken with tuberculosis, dying…was giving a recital and the camera caught a drop of consumptive blood – in glorious technicolor – falling tragically on to the alabaster ivory keys of the piano. Very dramatic. Memorable…And on the way home George's Mum looked down on him with tears in her eyes and said, "Oh George," she said, "look what'll happen to you. You'll hae to stop playin' that piano…" Well fortunately he didn't and although he has had a few health problems over the years these have not included any chest or lung complaint.

My favourite story of Buff's is just one of the hazards of being a public figure, because that's become your job. We were at the King's in Glasgow and a gentleman came round back-stage after the show to see Mr Hardie. He didn't introduce himself but said, "Ha, ha, you'll remember me from the old days". Well Buff had no idea, but didn't like to admit it because it is discourteous not to remember people. So a little game ensued in the course of which Buff said, "Wait a minute – it is the beard that's putting me off – I can't see through the whiskers and you've maybe lost a bit on the top…"

And the chap said, "Come on now, surely you remember… Stewart Park…" And Buff said, "Of course, Stewart, good to see you…"

And the reply came, "No, no, I'm not Stewart Park – that's where we used to play when we were kids".

For once Buff was at a loss for words – and that's probably the point I have reached now…or if not at a loss for words, at a loss for time which must be pressing on – and as you know there is a time for everything.

"However, if you have any questions I'd be delighted to answer them."

So ended the talk and so began the questions from the audience. Very often it *would* have been more appropriate for the questions to come from *me to* the audience, such as, Why the awkward silence? Why the shuffling of feet?' However, there was one question which tended to crop up: "Why the name Scotland The What?" And the answer is to be found in Chapter 18, under *The Scottish Plumber,* which makes clear the attitude of my friends and myself to the popular tartan culture of that time. In addition to Andy Stewart's numbers, there was an even better known one (lyric by Cliff Hanley) called *Scotland The Brave.*

To a sceptic like myself this was an outrageous claim. Brave indeed! And what else? The thought process – in which there is a touch of indignation as well as a question – invited the response 'Scotland The What?' and I put that forward as the title for an early Aberdeen Revue Group show. Understandably, it was not accepted because the show covered a wide range of topics of which the subject raised by the question was only one.

Well, the title Scotland The What? was forgotten for several years, until we went to the Fringe in 1969 when it seemed to fit the bill. And this time Buff, George and James were happy with the idea and the rest is…well, not important enough for real history, but certainly significant enough to be explained in the context of this personal chronicle.

5. In Urina Veritas

"Let's do a show"
— I said to Buff and George

You probably won't have noticed, dear reader — and there is no reason why you should — that there were a couple of quite important omissions in the last chapter. These were the failure to follow up the reference to the Aberdeen University Charities Show (to be called hereinafter the Students' Show) without which STW? would never have come into being, and also how we came to make the decision to go to the Edinburgh Festival Fringe. Here's how I remember things…

"Starting is easy," as I quoted in the Introduction; the quote this time is, "Let's do a show," which is what they used to say in lesser Hollywood musicals. "Just the three of us, on the Fringe at the Edinburgh Festival."

It was late May 1968 and Buff, George and I were walking home just a little bit tipsy in the small hours, James having no doubt stayed on at the party to conduct the community singing.

We had been attending a re-union of the Students' Show which the four of us had written, composed, produced and directed for the students that year. The title was *Running Riot* and it had been a hugely enjoyable experience to see the students doing *their* stuff doing *our* stuff at HMT.

That had given me the bug to perform again, prompting the outburst to which George responded immediately. "Great!" he said.

Buff was pretty quick too. "Well…" he said cannily – and for him that

was wild enthusiasm. The drink and the night air must have got to him. In fact they must have got to all of us, because we immediately felt the urge to seal our agreement by peeing jointly and severally into the adjacent hedge. The fact that the hedge bordered the chimpanzee section of the local zoo seemed appropriate, but it was probably just a coincidence that the place closed down not long afterwards mainly on hygienic grounds.

Exterior of Aberdeen Zoo – fortunately not showing protagonists in story.

So, in micturation, was STW? conceived. Not that we had a name for the show then and the birth didn't take place for another fifteen months, as already described. However, the next beginning that deserves far more than just a passing mention is the Students' Show.

6. The Students' Show

"Tonight Alfred, we have one and fourpence-ha'penny."
—A line from *Easter Fare,* the 1952 show

Buff Hardie and I first met in the Students' Show during the Easter holidays in 1952. At least I think so — that's when he registered with me anyway, though there might have been a passing encounter through a mutual friend Eddie Fraser in the quad at King's in the previous term.

Although Buff is only a couple of years older than I, he was an Olympian figure to the wines and spirits of the cast. These included the Men's Chorus, which included at the tail-end a couple of mates and myself who had joined for a lark over the holidays.

If ever there was a misnomer it was Men's Chorus. As first year students we were little more than half-overgrown schoolboys and the word 'chorus' implies a degree of harmony in song or dance not possessed by a bunch of tone-deaf clodhoppers. This was a stage Buff somehow managed to bypass in a previous year. He oozed star quality, and by this time he had also attained the dizzy heights of script and lyric writer, denoting awesome cleverness. He and the rest of the production team were too grand to mix with the *hoi poloi,* but occasionally he would nod or grunt the time of day and these dour acknowledgements were pearls to treasure.

The name of that first show in which we both appeared was *Easter Fare* and fifty-eight years on, we can still bawl out some of the numbers from it if the moon is in the right quarter. I had only one line – "Tonight Alfred, we have one and fourpence-ha'penny." – in a sketch which was a take-off of *Have a Go*, a popular radio programme of the day, but I was so bowled over by the spirit of the whole thing that I could not wait for the following Easter to come.

This time I did rather better in the auditions for the sketches and this time too, I had got to know Buff better. I shall never forget doing the audition for one sketch in particular. It was called *The Twa Tecs* and my part called for the portrayal of a dim-witted policeman. That I didn't find this too difficult was not only to do with type-casting, but also because I was able to reproduce the voice and dialect of an old worthy in Torphins, the little village up Deeside where I had spent every summer holiday for umpteen years. I also over-emphasised the slight speech defect from which the old worthy suffered, not to mock the afflicted, but in a newly-discovered desire to 'get the laughs'.

Buff Hardie certainly laughed anyway, so did the producer and I got the part. It was all very thrilling and when we got into the theatre and there was laughter from a real live audience, that was even more thrilling.

Not just one audience. A whole week of audiences. Huge audiences. In the early Fifties television had not reached the North-East of Scotland and cinemas and theatres flourished. Also the *Students' Show* was a local institution, an occasion every Easter at HMT when Town and Gown really did meet. This is not the place to discuss its contribution to the social fabric of the North-East, but in summary it had started shortly after World War I as a fund-raising effort for local hospitals (no NHS in those days) and had attracted a lot of talent. Eric Linklater was involved in the early days and then a little later Andrew Cruickshank, and over the years it had bred its own stars who were popular locally.

As a small boy taken to the theatre by my parents I used to fall about as much at the Students' Show comedians – such names as Vincent Park, Kiki McKay and Bert Crow – as I did at Abbot & Costello and Laurel & Hardy at the pictures. All of these I saw and enjoyed long before the great Harry Gordon, whose palmy days at the Beach Pavilion were before the war and who did not appear at HMT until well after that.

In later years Buff and I discovered that we shared these same boyhood influences, to which should be added the wireless programmes featuring

Awa ye feel, awa ye feel! I dinna like ye!

such names as Tommy Handley, Rob Wilton, and a bit later Tony Hancock, Kenneth Williams and Jimmy Edwards, whom we met when he became Rector of the University. There won't be too many who remember him now, but Jimmy Edwards, D.F.C., M.A. (Cantab.) was very big in his day, and when he came to see the Show in April 1954 – a revue called *Laughing at Life* which I had had a lot to do with – there was a terrific buzz amid cast and crew.

Unfortunately the excitement didn't extend to Jimmy. When he came backstage afterwards on the opening night, I was introduced to him. He made no bones about his opinion of one of my character parts.

"What the hell was that all about?" he said, handlebar moustache bristling, "I couldn't understand a word you were saying."

Of course he was quite right. Trying to be too damn clever, I had contrived a strange eldritch croak for playing an elderly lamplighter and Mr Edwards was not alone in being baffled by it. No wonder there were no laughs. Next night and for the rest of the week I reverted to a more normal Doric voice and the sketch went fine. A lesson learnt. Comprehensibility essential – naturalism less so – a difficult balance achieved by too few of the modern generation, a complaint also made by

Sir Peter Hall in *The Times* just a day or so after this was written.

Funnily enough, the high-pitched screech abandoned after one night in 1954 was brought into service again after nearly forty years – but this time in avian form. The concept of a Doric Parrot appealed to audiences and the feathered brute took me over – and disgracefully over the top during some performances, notably when there might have been a hen-party in the house (a hen-house?). I/he ('cos the Parrot, despite the mezzo-soprano squawk, was definitely, aggressively masculine) rose to the challenge of all that daft wifie helpless screaming. And rose. And rose. And rose yet again. "Awa' ye feel, awa' ye feel. Ye're a besom. Ye're a besom. Ye're a besom." High decibel repeated verbal abuse went down a ton in the henhooses.

But I am getting too far ahead of myself – back to the beginning of the Students' Show and Buff who was its main influence throughout the Fifties, not so much as a performer (although he is wickedly funny in certain parts) but as a sketch-writer and lyricist.

There was a reminder last year of just how accomplished even Buff's early lyrics were. A retired music lecturer living in Devon got in touch as he was researching the career of a late colleague, Philip Lord, who had been at Aberdeen for five years or so and had worked with Buff in a couple of shows. This necessitated the expiscation from a sea of forgotten material some delightful versifying, one beautifully-crafted, witty piece called *Musical Trio* coming particularly to mind.

It is no exaggeration to say that even from those early days as a student Mr Hardie was writing clever, clever stuff, way up there with that of Flanders & Swann, Rodgers & Hart, Lesser & Lowe, more recently Kit and the Widow – even Bacharach & David, Tom Lehrer, Coward, Porter, and when on the top of his form, Stephen Sondheim.

Praise indeed, you may say, to be expected from a prejudiced partner and pal – and doubtless as a North-Easter you're entitled to be sceptical. But I, too, am an N-E man, yielding to no-one in healthy scepticism and I would like to put on record my forecast that Buff's lyrics will be STW?'s greatest legacy. Long after our sketches and monologues, the videos, CDs and all the rest of it, are rightly forgotten, eager academics, post-graduate keenos in social history local and national, will be digging in the archives, putting together the collected pieces and doing PhDs on the great man's contribution to the life and times of Scotland in the second half of the 20th Century.

And it all began in the *Students' Show*. But how was it that this infuriatingly reserved young man, so lacking in the slightest degree of pushiness, and devoid of enthusiasm for anything other than English cricket, Scottish rugby and Aberdeen Football Club, deigned to get involved in such an extravagant business as the *Students' Show*?

Step forward his great friend and classmate in the Classics Department, one J. Edward Fraser C.B.,M.A.(Aberd) B.A.(Cantab), an Aberdeen Grammar School hero of mine – the only school hero I ever had who was not a sportsman. In fact, I suspect he was a duffer at Sport, except in the rather arcane field of fencing (and of course you cannot have a field without fencing ...sorry) at which, in the face of not very fierce competition, he was apparently less incompetent.

But what everybody admired about Eddie was that his braininess, an unfortunate condition usually to be deplored, was redeemed by decency and the common touch. I knew him pretty well from schooldays in very different guises. As leader, no less, of the Curlew Patrol of the 1st (AGS) Scout Troop he was kind to the small fry, of which I was the lowliest of the lower ranks, and didn't swear much at all, but was tolerant of his thicker peers, who did.

His saintly mien was no doubt one reason why he was cast in the main part of Thomas a Becket in the school play at St Machar's Cathedral in his final year. He was blessed, too, by a terrific memory and a gentle voice which he applied to the wordy vastness of T.S. Eliot's poetry, culminating in the most beautiful performance.

I was in that production too, in a minor role, but noticeable enough for one wag – who shall be nameless – to express the view that the play was aptly entitled *Murder in the Cathedral*. That may have been a tragedy, but it was comedy which was to bring us together in the Students' Show; for Eddie it was who, having been bold enough to go into it in his first year, engineered the conscription of Buff in his second year and almost certainly, with a genial twinkle, gave me the notion the year after that. It was almost certainly Eddie Fraser, therefore, who with no thought of the consequences, brought Buff and myself into the same circle.

7. Nature v Nurture
Case Precedent and An Early Struggle

**"Between the two of them Steve and Professor McRitchie
knew everything there was to know about Conveyancing.
Professor McRitchie knew all the answers and
Steve knew all the questions."**

Thus spake the proposer of one of the toasts when Eva and I got married on 4th October 1958. The cheek of the remark was pretty accurate and got a huge laugh – a sure indication of the firm friendship which I had been fortunate enough to form with Buff – for he it was, of course, who was purveyor of the merry quip.

Yes, I was a poor student, scraping through to graduation by the skin of my teeth and ultimately, I suspect, through the sympathy of the examiners whom I had worn into submission. Not that I didn't put in a bit of effort to even the most boring of subjects, of which there were too distressingly many, but I was not helped by involvement with the *Students' Show* and other extra-mural diversions. I really did try, but too little too late, and my memory just was not retentive enough to cope with that desperate last minute cram which enabled classmates no more diligent than I, but with much greater legal aptitude, to pass their exams first time.

If the examiners had not been kind, if they had not turned a blind eye to the obvious, that I was hardly God's gift to the Law, what might have happened? Ironically, the shock might have been beneficial, because I would have been forced to look for employment in something I liked and for which any abilities I did have were better suited. And what I did like, of course, was comedy and the stage. By the time I left university I had done five *Student Shows* and felt comfortable doing the odd bit of comic writing and in looking for the comic dimension of the parts in which I was cast. Audience laughter was the goal and scoring a goal is a thrill. I don't think I ever reached the point of being stage-struck and obsessive, but I got a lot of satisfaction from connecting with an audience. Their laughter was addictive and the pursuit of that addiction could have led to some sort of success in the professional theatre and its offshoots.

Or not. Show business is notoriously fickle and though I sometimes wonder what might have been, there is absolutely no doubt in my mind that it was for the best that I struggled through these bloody re-sits and finally got my solicitor's practising certificate. What an achievement! I was far more euphoric reaching that hard, unnatural pinnacle than basking in the limelight, laughter and applause of a packed theatre. That was easy. A thrill sure – and there were some great nights and wonderful memories – but easy by comparison with something that really had to be fought for.

There are two strands to follow from this rather solipsistic raid on the memory bank; they overlap one on the other and are both crucially relevant to STW? The first historical strand is that, having succeeded in getting into the slow lane of the solicitor branch of the legal profession, I found that it was not in the least bit humdrum. It was all about real life and real people. You never knew what was coming next. Or who. Or why. It could be nerve-wracking and stressful, but you soon discovered that ninety per cent of the stuff needed for the exams was scarcely needed at all in practice, most of which was to do with common sense and getting on with people – colleagues, staff, other lawyers, clients – particularly clients, to whom it was a matter of pride to give a decent service.

Luck came into it, too. After a few false starts I became an assistant in a small but respected firm where, due to death and retiral, I found myself senior partner only a couple of years after joining. Being thrown in at the deep end meant a lot of pressure and hard work, but also led to a deal more self-confidence and the elbow-room to organise things in such a way as to permit this hobby of writing and performing comedy, a hobby which gained immeasurably from the daily hurly-burly of the law and the constant contact with interesting people and situations.

Just off the top of my head, it is unlikely that such key items in the STW? repertoire as the old farmer making his will, the Baillie in the District Court, and the Mourners at the crematorium would have appeared if the law examiners had told me to run off and join the circus, or at least a drama school. And it is unlikely, too, that the events of Chapter One would have taken place that led me to think that it might be worth writing this book.

8. Formation of a Partnership
Hardie and Robertson

> **"Would you be interested in having a go at writing together?"**
>
> — Myself to Buff

The second strand, intertwined with working for a living in the real world and the resultant memory store of characters and situations, is all to do with a gentleman already introduced. Several times. And rightly so. He is part and parcel of most of the pages in this book, both as best friend and writing partner, senior in ability as well as years, who will be sensitive to every nuance and the smallest detail.

Hardly surprising. William Dunbar Hardie and I have been writing together for nearly fifty years now and I claim therefore, not too unreasonably, to know a wee bit about his approach to, his ideas on and opinions of comedy, its heroes and its villains. And various other aspects of show business about which we've talked a lot and which gave rise to one of his brilliant parodies regarding the participation and oddish involvement of S.T.W?

To Irving Berlin's tune:

The miserable matinees in Airdrie or Troon
Far naebody can understand us richt.

The Mondays in Methlick, the Sundays in Scone,
The Chinese meals at twelve o' clock at nicht.
The bloomin' nuisance pittin' on make-up
That's when my dermatitis plays me up.
We've no business in Show Business
We're too long in the tooth.
Show biz folk are young and sharp and trendy
We're jist squares – we're no hypoten-use.
It's nae much fun to be the geriatric
In a theatric-
Al boarding hoose…

And so splendidly on – though difficult to learn.

Actually we never did play Airdrie or Troon, but in the early days the prospect of doing so would have had a certain exotic appeal, living as we did in our own comfort zone of Aberdeen an' twelve or even fifty mile roon. And Buff would have taken a lot of persuading to leave that comfort zone in which we first started.

Naturally it was I who had the effrontery to put the question, "Would you be interested in having a go at writing together?" And presumably out of a polite reluctance to say "No", Buff's fulsome response was something like, "Well, we could give it a try…"

The location of this exchange I don't remember, but the date was January 1961, after Eva and I had come home from London where we had been living after National Service. We'd bumped into Buff and learned of his disappointment that the Aberdeen Revue Group, of which he was a key member, was in danger of breaking up. Founded three years previously by Buff and several others of like mind and humour – who shared an unwillingness to give up on youthful folly, now that they had begun serious careers – this gang of talented young people had enjoyed great success with shows in the old ballroom of the Music Hall.

In fact, Eva was an early recruit to the Revue Group before she decided to devote all her spare time to an exclusive counselling service which she had established. This she conducted by correspondence, her sole client being a woebegone National Serviceman under the cosh of square-bashing at Catterick – Signalman Robertson S.A.C.23434656.

I had been disappointed to have missed out on the beginnings of the Revue Group because of Her Majesty's prior claim on my attentions;

Writing script is such hard work.

when we returned to Aberdeen, the chance of cadging a late invitation to join was a great consolation after our London adventure had not worked out quite as we had hoped. I would have been happy to have been a performer only, but one of the reasons for the dissolution of the Revue Group was the departure of Buff's original writing partner, a very nice guy called Alfie Wood, with whom he'd written shows during his National Service.

It seemed to me the natural way to break the awkward silence which followed the announcement of Alfie's departure was to venture, tentatively, the question which appears at the top of this chapter. Thus it was that Buff and I started writing together, and Eva and I became members of the revived Revue Group and formed lifelong friendships.

We differ, Buff and I, on what was the first thing we ever wrote. He thinks it was our Bruce and the Spider sketch. I think it was the Town Councillor giving his prize-giving speech[1]. Or was it the other way round?

No matter, it was one of these and we wrote it for a show in the Spring of 1961 called *Come What May*, performed in the Revue Group's old

[1] See Chapter 17, Item 13.

haunt, the ballroom of the Music Hall. The cast was Anne Logan (née Brand), Anne McWilliam, Joy Scaling, Glenis Wallace, Buff Hardie, Jabez Bruce, Derek Brechin – oh yes, and myself.

Or was that – it is so long ago – the cast of the second show, *Something Else,* a year or so later? Or the third, *You Name It,* a couple of years after that? Or the last one *Going, going…* in 1967, by which time some performers had been replaced by other highly talented folk such as Margaret Hardie (née Simpson), Jimmy Anderson, Quentin Cramb, Eva Robertson (née Stephen), George Reid, Douglas Kynoch and Rose McBain.

It is also impossible to forget Musical Director, pianist and composer George Donald, his delightful accomplice Muriel Sturrock and, indisputably, our overall Director and general factotum extraordinaire, James Logan – a most happy breed, some of whom are sadly gone far too early, but of whom Eva and I have such happy memories.

The demands of young families and day jobs really did bring the Revue Group to an end this time, however, with *Going, going…* following which everyone was supposed to settle down to respectable normality. After the salad days there was a fear that the salad might be getting limp because of exposure. But complete domesticity was not to be, not for some of us anyway, who could not quite bring ourselves to say, after *Going, going…* – Gone!

A bit of extra money is always welcome for young marrieds and luckily Anne, James, Buff, George and I were all being offered, jointly or severally, fee-paying engagements – even (big deal) by B.B.C. Scotland and Grampian Television. Anne was seriously in demand, mostly sharing with her sister Laura a successful singing career, but also hosting and singing solo in a TV series of her own for the Beeb called *Twixt Dee and Don.*

No doubt it was because of our local track record that Buff, George, James and I were approached by the Students' Show people to put together a production for their 1968 show. *Running Riot,* already mentioned as the catalyst for S.T.W? and the Edinburgh Festival Fringe, merits an even more special place because of its star without whom, playing the main comic part, we did not want to be involved. This was tricky because George Reid, the main man, was no longer a student at Aberdeen University. He was now doing a Ph.D. at King's College, London, and there was an unwritten rule that the Show was for Aberdeen University students only.

Aberdeen Revue Group 1967, left to right: George Donald, Quentin Cramb, Buff and Margaret Hardie, Steve Robertson, George Reid, Rose McBain, Douglas Kynoch and Anne Logan.

PHOTO: ABERDEEN JOURNALS

Ah well, rules are made to be broken. We got our way, creating a precedent for many others in later years, and George made the show in the role of Baillie Douglas Dawson, Councillor, with a finger in a puckly pies, wearer of numerous hats. The first one was that of gas inspector, his daytime job, and I can still see in my mind's eye George delivering his accusatory line, "There's an affa smell o' gas aboot this place..." in the thickest Aberdeen accent. Although Buff was the first to play the character of the pompously dodgy councillor, and do it extremely well, George somehow added another layer of authenticity.

George was a joy to write for and to work with, a lovely guy who died far too young in 2000 after a distinguished career with the British Council and the University of Lagos. His passing was desperately sad, but at least he ensured that the councillor character would live on, played thereafter by Buff in every S.T.W? show we ever performed, only his name being changed to that of Councillor Alexander Swick[2].

Although the good councillor hasn't appeared on stage for quite a number of years now, he continues to grace the pages of *Leopard* magazine every month in cartoon form. Happily this means that Buff and I have to get together at least once a month for writing purposes, the only trouble being that the writing bit gets in the way of a good gossip and catch-up on the affairs of Aberdeen Football Club or the Scottish Rugby Union. Cricket I discourage, but am not always successful until I permit the eyes to glaze over and the head to nod, then Buff gets the message and we go for lunch.

Sir Ian Wood (centre, back) – What a coup for us. But was he wearing dark glasses because he did not want to be recognised?

---

[2] 'Swick', a word indigenous to the North-East of Scotland, means "to cheat or deceive in a trivial kind of way". It can also be a noun however, as in "What a swick you are avoiding paying your bus fare".

9. An Earlier Partnership
Hardie and Donald

"Hullo, hullo – good to see you!"
— George Donald

George is a brick – everybody whose path he has crossed even fleetingly in his 76 packed years and whom he has probably forgotten – knows that he is a brick in the human sense, albeit with the occasional straw of unpunctuality. But I am talking of his qualities as a really solid, professional brick, an integral, indispensable brick in the foundations of S.T.W?

After all, George had been in the Revue Group which begat S.T.W? long before I had and, even before that, had had a connection with the

---

[1] So many people knew George that it was impossible for him to remember them all. Buff and I were amazed at the number of former pupils, relatives, friends and professional contacts who would turn up or "come round" to say hullo. This could be difficult for him if he was unsure of his visitor but he always coped manfully with that very characteristic friendly greeting. One famous former pupil, however, he could not forget and when we were needing a bit of extra publicity one summer season George said, "Leave it to me, lads. I'll easily give Ian Wood a ring and see if he'll get his photo taken with us." And George did. And Ian did. What a coup! And I don't think we ever thanked Sir Ian properly for a gesture of such personal magnanimity.

Students' Show which largely begat the Revue Group. The word 'connection' needs to be explained. With the encouragement of Reg. Barrett-Ayres, Musical Director of the 1954 Show called *Laughing at Life*, George had submitted a couple of tunes. One was accepted by Reg who,

George – a passion for music

I well remember, sang the praises of this country loon who could not be in the show because he had to go home to Huntly for a holiday job during the Easter rehearsals.

But George had written his song with Reg and got a credit and made the connection, and that is how I knew his reputation as a big talent before we met. Although we had been at University at the same time – he was just one year behind – and had almost certainly passed each other in the quad, or the library, even at the occasional class (though I confess my visits to the Arts classes were extremely occasional) we only met through the Revue Group. And strange as it seems now, after such a close friendship of donkey's years, that was not long enough to merit an invitation to his wedding in the summer of 1961. This was to Isabelle, daughter of his French professor, a liaison which came as a pleasant surprise to Eva and myself. We had both known Izzy for years, in Eva's case at school and in mine at university where she was a very lively spirit, chattering her way through medicine without apparent effort and taking part in lots of social activities, which included doing make-up backstage in the show.

George's passion for music, especially the piano, was well exemplified by the Reg Barrett-Ayres connection. He may have been doing his degree in French and German, because he had been advised that was the prudent and orthodox thing to do for a career in education, but his first love was music and he was never away from the Music Department where he fell under the spell of the great R.B.A.

And Reg was a great guy… a seminal influence on Buff and myself, too, in our Student Show days. When he died – another far too soon – I yielded to the urge to write an appreciation of the man as I knew him and I sent it rather hesitantly to the P&J who were kind enough to give it space.

Tribute to varsity's Reader in Music

The death of Mr Reginald Barrett-Ayres (61), Reader in Music at Aberdeen
University, is a loss not only to the university and the community but to the many
friends he made among students down through the years.

In this tribute, a former student reflects the endearing personality of the man of
music whose approach to young people will be long remembered.

WHEN you know about only a small part of someone's life – and that was
for a short time long ago – the justification for an unsolicited
pronouncement of this kind has to be considerable. Reg's impact – even
the most fleeting contact – was not only considerable, it was electric with
extraordinary possibilities and that is the justification for this profile to add
to the formal tributes; and that would be the justification also for the same
kind of response from any one of hundreds of students who came under his
extra-mural influence in the Students' Shows of the Fifties and Sixties.

The Reg whom most of us will look back on from those days was a fun
figure – but much respected fun. The laughter had much to do with his
philosophical perspective on life's buffetings, but it was mostly for physical
reasons. Reg was on the short side, rather roly-poly in those days, in a sere
sweater of ancient and notable line which did nothing for him, having once
probably belonged to an Iona fisherman who must surely have lived last
century – and died still wearing it. And to say that Reg was as blind as a bat
as he peered nonchalantly at you through his prejudices – of which he had
one or two – is to be not very complimentary to the bat.

However, it is also to ignore the acuteness of his other senses and
sensibilities and in these lay the reason for the respect. The musical ear got
him on the right wave-length very quickly; the sixth sense redeemed the
dim sight.

If the senses were sharp, the appetites were sharper. He had an
enormous capacity for enjoyment exceeded only by hunger to give more
than he took from life, even of those bits which were alien to him and
which might be inimical to his optical frailty.

The definitive reminiscence is of the scene after a long evening's
rehearsal in the old gymnasium in the bowels of Marischal College. A game
of soccer would sometimes start spontaneously and it was not uncommon
to see Reg in passionate, un-coordinated engagement, a bottle of export in
one hand, a pie in the other, the ball all too briefly at his despairing feet, his
waiting cigarette smoking in an ashtray nearby, and cheered on by a crowd

of admiring chorus girls.

The immediacy of these pleasures and the human involvement was all and he gave his all to our enrichment and privilege.

Reg often interrupted a lunchtime sherry in the Kirkgate to remember that he was due to play at a wedding ten minutes ago and a flurried exit to the bus or taxi, or just a friendly passing car would then get him out to King's, gingerly to ascend the organ loft in time to put his own stamp on the conclusion of solemnities.

When friends were involved he would embellish the music with his own grace notes; soaring above the Handel would be a snatch of *McGinty's Meal and Ale*, or a tinkling ditty, maybe one of his own lesser works, known to the happy pair. It was all an in-joke, his own compliment and celebration of the day. When my wife and I got married he got the wrong tune for one of the hymns we had chosen, but the grace notes were brilliantly, movingly, there. Reg never forgot the grace notes. It was not in his nature ever to forget the grace notes.

And Reg it was, as an original member of the Revue Group, who brought George along in the early days. Having to bow out due to other pressures, Reg left George in charge of the musical side of things. That meant that he composed any original music that was needed and that in turn meant working with Buff, already a prolific lyric writer.

So, you see, Buff and George have actually been partners longer than Buff and I. But theirs has been a different kind of partnership, not only in terms of its end result, which is musical as opposed to verbal, but also in relation to working methods. George and Buff worked at a distance, Buff crafting pointed lyrics then sending them to George to conjure up a tune to catch the mood of the words. The pair of them then got together to sort out the result of the joint enterprise.

Buff and I, though, were closeted together for hour upon hour, day after day. The process of writing a sketch would usually begin most agreeably with a drink, in the early days a beer or two in the pub. Later when we had gone full time it would be a dram or two at home when, having hit upon a subject, we would worry it to bits, looking at it from any and every angle, trying as we did so – and finding the funny threads unravelling – to make each other laugh. That was the easy part.

At least at our next session we had our slightly inebriated notes to start from, rather than the dreaded sheet of blank paper, but trying to make a coherent whole of these was the hardest part. Not quite so hard would be the refining business of looking the piece over and coming at it afresh after a day or two, making an objective appraisal and probable adjustment.

The fourth part of the process was a bit harder again – exposure to the eagle eye of James our Director, who would leave us alone for a few days and then breeze in at coffee time, perhaps interrupting a period of gentle contemplation or a well-earned break to scan the newspapers between our comedic labours. And he would proclaim animatedly, "Morning, lads! Hard at it! What have you got for us today then?"

Such high octane energy polluting the peace and quiet of an innocent morning could have resulted in a punch on the nose, but James was quite right, of course. We needed a kick in the pants to shake us out of our torpor and he would then listen po-faced as we read to him our latest efforts. "Great, lads," he might then say most courteously," but you could maybe do with pruning it a bit."

Editing would then follow, each line being debated until a consensus was reached. Even then James wouldn't be entirely satisfied and would deliver himself, rather less politely, of what was his shorthand for a few passable jokes, finishing with a very broad effect intended to culminate in an explosion of audience laughter.

"All you're wanting is half-a-dozen cripplers and then finish with a couple of sausages and a knickers."

This was the language of high culture. No wonder James was at one time on the Arts Council of Great Britain and Vice-Chairman of the Scottish Arts Council. He certainly picked out our strengths and weaknesses, knew what your average audience would find funny – and his editing skills and judgment unquestionably improved the end product.

But I digress. This chapter is supposed to be about George, both solo and in partnership with Buff. In each capacity he demonstrated the most extraordinary versatility of talent. In the days of the old Revue Group he was in the pit, not in the limelight. Having happily composed and arranged to order the music for the show, he was then just as happy to be the accompanist for other people's performances. It was not until S.T.W? went to the Fringe that he aspired – at his friends' request – to join them on stage and proved what a winner he was at the simultaneous business of playing and singing.

That is a most marvellous skill and George mastered it in no time as if to the manner born. As I write I can still remember his very first number –

a Scottish version of Cole Porter's *Let' Do It* – updated with topical words by Buff, musical arrangement, witty accompaniment and performance by George. It was a virtuoso rendering of sophistication and charm to which I listened in the wings every night with huge admiration and pride to be associated in this fantastic enterprise with these wonderfully clever guys who were my friends. Actually, forty-odd years on I still feel the same.

However auspicious a debut that was, it was no more than a modest hors d'oeuvres in the great spread of George's performing career. As we developed the show from one hour to two and from wee halls to big theatres, it became clear that for logistic as well as artistic reasons the evening would benefit from a solo piano spot which was a bit special and starry. In playing to our strengths, George was given full rein in what came to be called his 'Variations'.

What he did, for example, was to play well-known Scottish songs in the style of the classical composers – Beethoven, Handel, Mozart and so on – or famous classical pieces in the Scottish idiom. All the variations of the Variations worked splendidly and were George's own dazzling compositions with perhaps a wee injection from James, pretending he was the punter in the stalls, to help make them popularly accessible.

George's glorious and unique apogee, however, achieved in our *Final Fling*, was when he played and sang *Figaro*. This is the famous aria *Largo al Factotum* from the *Barber of Seville* by Rossini which, sung in the orthodox way by any of the great tenors has a paucity of words, but a plethora of notes – very difficult indeed. But Buff cottoned on to another possibility – not 'Figaro' but 'Figure O' – and created a parody of wondrous complexity, all to do with the three tenors, Pavarotti, Carreras and Domingo, coining in the cash; brilliant idea, brilliant lyric, but virtually impossible to articulate.

George, however, managed the impossible and in so doing succeeded in showing S.T.W? at its very best. I say 'its' not 'our' best advisedly, because I had no more hand in *Figaro* than I had had in any of George and Buff's songs. As I stood by the piano every night towards the end of the show listening to George doing his stuff, with Buff the wordsmith standing attentively between us, I used to marvel at the quality of what had been created. I had the same feeling as I had had at the Fringe all these years before.

I will say it again: I was just so proud to be associated with these marvellously talented guys who were my friends.

10. A Man of Magic

"O.K. lads – Fizz! Let's have a bit of joie!"

— James Logan

On one of those precious 48-hour passes home from Catterick in early 1958, Buff told me about starting the Revue Group with a few other like-minded souls. One of the names he mentioned was a famous one: "We've also got Jimmy Logan," he said.

"Of course," I said. "And Stanley Baxter and Kenneth McKellar."

"No," he said, deadpan as usual, "they're a bit busy – and so are Tony Hancock and Jimmy Edwards."

"Oh, that's a pity," I said, "I'd have liked to see Edwards and Hancock doing a Doric double act."

"Oh well, never mind," he said. "At least Jimmy Logan is bringing his girl-friend with him and she's a singer. Her name is Anne Brand."

It took a while for the penny to drop. There was a genuine confusion between Jimmy Logan, Scotland's most famous entertainer of the day, and Jimmy Logan, research chemist at the Macaulay Institute of Soil Research who, as it happened, also dabbled in a bit of light entertainment and in later years, for the purpose of joining Equity, was obliged to use his formal Christian name, James, to distinguish him from his namesake, whose real name was actually Jack Short!

Anyway, our Jimmy as a young man was in concert parties as the conjurer, which doesn't sound much when you say it quickly – a trifle trivial and superficial perhaps – but when you think about it, the word indicates uplifting qualities which were to be of massive benefit to S.T.W?. A conjurer worth his salt has great skills – digital, verbal, presentational. He's light of touch in every sense. He knows about smoke and mirrors and keeping an audience intrigued. If he's any good at all he's a people person and has a sense of humour as quick as his fingers. These are unlikely characteristics for a back lab. boffin, but Jimmy had them all, plus, plus. I have no idea what he was like in the day job – no doubt precision and accuracy were required there, too – but he was an absolute natural for show business, a true conjurer of miracles. He was magic.

When James died in November 1993, Buff gave at the funeral a most moving address which he has kindly given me permission to reproduce here.

James Logan: A Tribute by Buff Hardie

A few years ago, I sought James' advice when I found myself in a situation in some respects similar to this one. I had been invited to give the address at the Gordon's College Founder's Day ceremony, and I was a little concerned to know what to say on what was a solemn occasion. Discussing this little local difficulty with James, I said to him, "The ceremony takes place in a church; is it appropriate for the audience to laugh?" To which he replied, "Just use some of your usual material, William, and you won't have any problem".

So is laughter appropriate today? Surely not, one would think. Because today we mourn. We mourn the passing of one taken too soon from a world to which he still had much to give, too soon from his friends whose lives were enriched by his friendship, too soon above all from his family in whom he had such pride.

And yet, is laughter inappropriate today? For as we mourn, we remember, and I hazard a guess that there are few here today whose best memories of James are not associated with laughter. He was a great bringer, a great raiser of laughter.

Only last week, when Steve and I visited him for what turned out to be the last time, he somehow found the strength to make us laugh with a lovely story of his early theatre-going – of how, as a teenage member of an audience at the Palladium, he confounded Leslie Welch, the

Uniquely, all in step, led by the Man of Magic. PHOTO: ABERDEEN JOURNALS

Memory Man, by asking who first had tossed the caber at the Braemar Gathering.

At his best, and in his pomp, his skill as a raconteur could reduce the most frosty-faced to helpless mirth. As many may know, but some may not, his earliest forays into show business were as conjurer-compère, in the days of innocence, pre-television, when the concert party was a vital element in the entertainment scene. And no-one who has heard it will ever forget his story of the lady contortionist – for there were such in those days – who, as the star attraction, was allocated the prime spot, just before the interval, but who, having reached the high point of her act, a hanky in her mouth, and her head located in what was a physically improbable position in relation to her legs, had to unravel herself ahead of schedule when James signalled to her from the wings that her audience had been totally lost to the more compelling attractions of three WRI ladies making a dramatic entrance from the back of the hall, bearing two vast teapots and a tray of bridies. Believe me, to sit with a glass of malt whisky in the hand, listening to James telling that story, playing simultaneously the parts of himself, the tea ladies, the contortionist, and at least half of the audience, was to live life at its most sublime.

It was perhaps his youthful hobby of conjuring that bred in him his love of the theatre, because illusion is at the heart of all good theatre. And his love of the theatre was insatiable. He would say, "I just love sitting in a darkened theatre waiting to be surprised".

But he was knowledgeable not just about the theatre, but across the whole spectrum of the Arts, and the obituaries in the Press this week have detailed his involvement, and listed his achievements, in the field of Arts administration – member of the Art Gallery Committee, long service on the Arts Centre Committee, founder Chairman of the Friends of the Art Gallery, administrator of the Maritime Museum Appeal, member and subsequently Vice-Chairman of the Scottish Arts Council, member of the Arts Council of Great Britain, culminating in the award of the O.B.E. in 1988.

As a theatre director, he had a gift for generating excitement in a cast – particularly of young people – and he had a talent for presenting to their optimum theatrical advantage the most unmalleable of performers. I speak from experience – they don't come much more unmalleable than me.

His contribution to whatever chemistry Scotland the What? has, was to make it look smooth, relaxed and effortless; and, as a ruthless but sharply perceptive script editor, to protect the show from the more self-indulgent excesses of its authors.

He was a man of strong opinions, not solely, but especially, in artistic matters. Indeed, he may very well even now be arguing with Scott Skinner about the tempo of a jig, or telling Shakespeare, how, by cutting a few hundred lines, he could make a really good play out of Hamlet.

In addition to his activities in the Arts scene, James was very active behind the scenes politically, in the service of the Labour Party in Aberdeen. One of his most satisfying achievements was to have contributed to Donald Dewar's victory in South Aberdeen in 1966, and as late as October of this year, as I watched the Conservative Party Conference with him on the telly, the crassness of some of the speakers produced from him a vigour of response that was more than all of medical science could achieve.

Coming from the hardship of a mining background, he never lost sight of the Labour Party's true mission as the protector of the have nots; and personally he devoted much time and unsung effort to the service of the disadvantaged, notably from his long-running contribution, latterly as its chairman, to the valuable achievements of Voluntary Service Aberdeen.

James was a terrific doer: a terrific doer himself, and a great energiser of others. Fizz he would ask for. And fizz he would invariably get. The obverse of this was that he was not the world's best delegator, tending to give instructions, then immediately carry them out himself before the recipient had got started.

There is little that is good that can come out of protracted terminal illness; over the past four months the large number of callers and visitors to 53 Fountainhall Road, from all walks of life, many from long distances, brought home to one how many people there were whose lives had been touched and whose respect and affection for him made them want to come and see him.

His was a full life, richly led and conveying riches to others, and shared with a wonderful woman. During the final harrowing stage of his illness, we, her friends, could only be helpless admirers of Anne's devoted and constant care, which enabled James to spend the end of his life in the home which they had created together and which he loved so much.

Some words in James' vocabulary recurred frequently. One of these was "quality". He liked quality whisky, quality food, quality theatre, quality movies, quality music, quality people. He married quality, and together he and Anne have produced quality, yea, even unto the next generation.

But sometimes when James used the word "quality" it had a concealed meaning, a hidden agenda. Over the years, George, Steve and I learned to know what he meant if he came into the dressing-room before a show and said, "You'll find it is a quality house this evening, lads". That meant it was sadly lacking in quantity. Today's gathering to honour his memory and celebrate his life is both quality and quantity. That was the kind of house James liked – and deserved.

– Buff Hardie, 1 December 1993

I have one more very personal recollection of events at the time of James' death. We heard of it when we were doing the show in Dundee. We were in the Bonar Hall, part of the University which therefore doesn't have happy associations for us. "The show must go on," is the great cliché, but never did it go on with more hidden sorrow than when we had just got the ghastly news. Never was James' own admonition, "Fizz – let's have a bit of joie," harder to follow.

My concentration went completely as that unruly mind of mine went a-meandering on to thoughts of James in my number where the old minister is doing a christening. It is a test for the memory even in the most favourable circumstances, and in a thinnish house carrying that stupid doll in my arms with the blotch on its nose and one of the eyes that didn't shut properly, I went to pieces. My mind went blank. Awful, awful dry. Panic. In an item due to last ten minutes, I had done about a minute-and-a-half when lightening struck. All I was able to do was cut to the end tag line, which must have been meaningless to the audience.

That was bad enough. Equally horrible was the fact that George, who was due on next, was in his dressing room unaware of the problem. Consequently there was the most embarrassingly, ghastly hiatus before he clattered breathlessly on to the stage, got to the piano and, fixing a mirthless rictus of a smile on a bemused house, got down to business with a rattle of duff notes. I console myself with the thought that such a disaster was in a way a tribute to James and the hold he had on my affections, but if he'd been directing that show he would have been furious. Or maybe not. Knowing James he would have been just as likely to dissolve in laughter and conjure up a comforting lie "Totally minor" was a characteristic brush-aside which might well have been followed by the classic summing up: "Well, that's Show Business".

Part Two

The Part-Time Years
1969-1982/83

Preface

"Well that's the end of the beginnings," as Winston Churchill nearly said, and there were a lot of digressions. "This tree has many branches," Graham Hunter our Business Manager always said when apologising in advance for a long diffuse story. And what follows – although largely chronological – may also become a bit diffuse, as one thing inevitably sparks off another and we will just have to see how it goes. However, a good enough start is our second visit to the Fringe a year after the first… and come to think of it, that was really another of the beginnings…

11. The Fringe leads to HMT

"Well, you've done two one-hour shows,
last year and this year. Why don't you put them
together and do an evening at H.M.T?"
— James Donald, Director of H.M.T.

Considering that H.M.T. was to become S.T.W?'s 'home' for the next 25 years, this invitation extended to us in the autumn of 1970 made our second visit to the Fringe a big success. But not an unqualified one.

Second time round we were much more comfortable in several ways. First of all we had a great back-stage team – John Duffus, George and Sheila Reid and Ian Reid (no relation) – sometime stalwarts all of the Students' Show. Now embarked on their careers, they were happy to be bullied by James to take some holiday time, just for a bit of a jolly in the Festival atmosphere and, as good friends, to give us support where needed.

We were also delighted to welcome back from the previous year our officer in charge of the box office, which took the form of a shoogly table in a draughty corner. Angela Hewitt was the gallant lady enlisted by James for this sometimes lonely duty which she discharged with charm and great good humour.

Another comfort was that of knowing exactly where we were to be doing the show and where we were to be staying. The venue was St. Mary's Cathedral Hall again, through the good offices of my Edinburgh colleague Bill Bryden, and the accommodation was a large flat half-a-mile away where there were real beds and a bathroom instead of sleeping bags and a guilty trip to the North British.

I shared a room with John Duffus whom I had first met when he had been Administrator of our show *Running Riot* a couple of years previously. Since then he had graduated with a First in Music and had had a spell as a trainee with the B.B.C. before deciding the Beeb was not for him and going to Scottish Opera, which was much more to his liking. John, who was steeped in classical music and had a love of the entertainment business generally, went on to enjoy a most unusual career organising concert tours in the Far East, including Bangkok and Hong Kong. That was where George, James, Anne and I met up with him in early 1991 when we were staying in the Mandarin Oriental Hotel there – a wee treat we had given ourselves coming home from Bangkok where we had been the guests of the St. Andrews Society, helping them celebrate Burns Night.

John had telephoned, apologising for not being able to spend longer than an hour with us because he was so busy; he duly turned up for a quick drink, bearing the evidence for his urgent departure. This took the form of a passport which he tantalisingly allowed us to look at – with awe, jaws dropping in amazement. It had been entrusted to him for the purpose of establishing his credentials in negotiating arrangements on behalf of his client. Apparently the Mandarin hotel, which we had found totally marvellous and which Anne had booked because she had read that it was "the best in the world," did not, according to John's client's management, come up to snuff.

Only half of the top floor was available for the party, including the Emperor's suite for the main man himself, the rest of the accommodation being elsewhere: the Hyatt, therefore, was the preferred choice. In neither case was payment required. The great man's presence was payment enough and indeed an honour for the establishment. The face on the passport was that of Luciano Pavarotti, someone not to be trifled with, even though he obviously did like his trifle, with or without extra custard, all preceded by heroic quantities of pasta.

But back to the 1970 Fringe. The show went smoothly after judicious cutting. The impersonation I did of Enoch Powell was the main victim. At the time Enoch was at the centre of public attention because of his

I have just remembered this one-and-only snap from the 1970 Fringe Show. From left to right are: Steve Robertson, George Donald, Buff Hardie, James Logan, John Duffus, Graham Hunter, George Reid and (kneeling) George's wife, Sheila. PHOTO: AUTHOR

"rivers of blood" speech, and the piece we wrote was supposed to be topical satire; but although I had worked at *it*, *it* didn't work for me. Or anyone. Oot.

A much more successful number – again featuring a famous figure of the day – was Colin Mitchell M.P., formerly Colonel 'Mad Mitch', whom we depicted addressing the House of Commons in military fashion as if on parade. "House of Commons, Attention. Now, I don't know what you think you're on, but you're a scruffy, idle, dozy lot." And so on, attacking the front benches of the day. "Take that pipe out of your mouth, Wilson. Get your eyebrows trimmed, Healey. What the hell are you grinning at, Heath?"[1]

Nobody remembers that sort of thing now, but both of these items exemplify rather an important point. When S.T.W? began on the Fringe we did not do any Doric material at all, assuming that it wouldn't be understood by Festival audiences. It was only later when we started playing H.M.T. that we introduced the North-East dialects, both country and town, that we came to be identified with. And here's another important point – basic ideas matter more than dialect – or any of the other bits that go into the jigsaw of a successful comedy number, including the look and sound of it, the words and music, the language and the very performance. All must get into a seamless, colourful whole, but if the original concept isn't right it is an uphill struggle. That's my opinion anyway. Such reviews as we got that fortnight were fine, except one which did rather qualify our positive feelings and cast a slight shadow over the whole enterprise since it appeared in *The Scotsman*. Albert Morris was not your usual critic. He was himself a humorist and as a regular columnist in the *Scotsman*, a writer of superb skills. He thrived, flourished and was almost over-nourished on words, using them with wit, delicacy and cunning. He was undoubtedly a master of his craft and it must be presumed that following the modest success we had enjoyed the year before, he had chosen or been chosen to go along and see what we were all about. And he did not care for us, as his piece demonstrates:

An extract from the programme by this indomitably cheerful three-man show states: 'They are using the same formula (as last year), the same hall, same prices… the same title, almost the same jokes'. Alas, it is palpably true and their previous success which they modestly describe as 'mild' may well be accorded to this production.

This is indeed sad, since the trio have obviously an impressive reservoir of talent and have engaging personalities, but at few points are they able to transcend material which is flimsy to the consistency of banality and hackneyed to the point of dreariness.

The revue tilts, sometimes with all the unsubtlety of a rhinoceros charge, at subjects which include politicians, education and the theatrical world, but the humour is often laboured and has a hammer-on-anvil effect where it should have been scalpel-sharp.

[1] Actually, we met Ted Heath during that Festival visit. There was a reception for all sorts of participants in the grand surroundings of the Caledonian Hotel and when we were introduced to the principal guest as the performers in a revue called STW? he reall did respond according to charicature with a mirthless laugh and a heaving of the shoulders.

Winner of the North-East Oscars 1979 "Intellectual alembic"?
Forget it – this was just dead funny and the audiences loved it.

Nevertheless, it is saved from the levels of sheer mediocrity by some
delightful music and astringent lyrics, facets which are an encouraging
pointer that this group could, by careful use of an intellectual alembic,
eventually distil a less coarse-grained (in the technical sense) show which
would be worthy of their abilities.

Ouch! Clearly no appreciation, was there, of there being any merit in
"cripplers, sausages or knickers"?

Maybe we got the last word. A long while later when we were full-
time and enjoying an autumn run at the Kings in Edinburgh, we were
interviewed by Allan Wright, highly respected as the main *Scotsman* critic
for many years. We went out for lunch with him and much enjoyed the
company of this most courteous and civilised gentleman. The gossip was
not at all bad either, the most memorable bit being that the review which
Albert Morris had written about us was the last one he ever did for the
Scotsman. Not only had we not liked it, apparently the Editor didn't care

for it either and forbade the erudite 'Bert', as Allan Wright charmingly called him, from attempting similar again.

He continued to sparkle in his weekly column, however, which was frequently such a clever joy that at least one collection was published in book form. I remember buying a copy for Buff as a Christmas present one year. It was intended as a private joke but, if I remember rightly, Buff thought it was in rather dubious taste.

Of course he's got no sense of humour.

12. H.M.T. as Home
– and the first away fixtures

"House Full"
– Poster outside H.M.T., May 1971

Thank you, Frank Matcham. Thank you for giving Aberdeen such a beautiful theatre. The great architect of more than a century ago had many other palaces of entertainment to his credit, but H.M.T. Aberdeen must surely be the best of the best. Not that I am biased... well, O.K., I am. Which is hardly surprising considering the happy times I have been lucky enough to experience there, both on stage and in the audience.

Our very first performance in H.M.T. took place in May 1971. It was a Friday and no doubt Jimmy Donald had a blank night or two at the end of a split week, but no matter, it was thrilling to be invited wearing the S.T.W? hat. Our last appearance there had been eight years previously in a show called *Element of Surprise* which we had written to mark the visit to Aberdeen University of the British Association (for the Advancement of Science).

That show had involved a large cast of former students. Now we were down to three – 'Three men, two chairs and one piano' as our billing put it – and we felt pretty intimidated as we looked out at the seriously large auditorium during the dress rehearsal. This was quite a leap from a two-three hundred seat church hall. All was well, however. We mastered our nerves, remembered our lines, didn't bump into the furniture – which admittedly was not too difficult since there was not much to bump into – and justified Jimmy Donald's faith in us to the extent that he allowed us to put on an extra performance on the Sunday, then said, "Well done. Come back and see me when you've got a new show together and I'll give you a week next time".

But "next time" was not to be for another two-and-a-half years – a gap which underlines the fact that S.T.W? was no more than a most enjoyable hobby for half of its lifetime. After all, we had demanding jobs and growing families and a new show meant starting with the dreaded blank sheet of paper.

Well, all right, the blank sheet of paper and a visit to the pub to bandy about ideas and situations that made us both laugh. And all right, that was enjoyable – if it had not been we wouldn't have bothered and in addition to the business of writing a new show for H.M.T. there was now the odd invitation from unexpected sources to perform the material we had already been doing.

The most interesting of these was from Antony Phillips, Director of the MacRobert Theatre at Stirling University, who must have spotted us at the Fringe. He was the first person out of Aberdeen to ask us to play an away fixture and he put us into his Studio Theatre, an intimate, arty kind of space which I suppose suited our scale of show, but in which I didn't feel too comfortable. Being part of a university, there were, naturally, quite a number of students about the place and being students they tended to be – well, studentish – restless, restive and rebellious of audience orthodoxy. In fact Stirling University about that time had a reputation for bad behaviour – shown particularly to the Queen when she performed the opening ceremony.

Anyway we must have done well enough to be asked back and to move into the main theatre, which proved much more agreeable since it attracted audiences of our own age group and older, the sensible citizens of Bridge of Allan, Dunblane and similar enclaves of civilised living. Anent which Antony Phillips seemed a fine and most helpful example. He was undoubtedly on the side of the angels, as we discovered in later years, but as a sensitive aesthete, definitely a man of high culture, his presence and conversation were a tad inhibiting for four middle-of-the-road, middle-

Showbiz happiness is…

aged, middle-brows like ourselves.

I remember him asking me about a sketch in which Buff and I played two old codgers, Mr Taylor and Mr Wallace, Aiberdeen mannies, sitting in front of a coal fire discussing its merits and then agonising over what next to speak about.

"Did you get the idea for that sketch from Flaubert's novel, *Bouvard et Pecuchet*, he said in all seriousness and it was truly a compliment that he should think I was that knowledgeable about French literature. Fortunately George was on hand as our French expert and he was able to flannel cheerfully while I remained dumb and felt extremely thick. When I recounted the incident later to Douglas Kynoch, who had permitted us to use a couple of his numbers for that show (and quite brilliant they were too), Doug's response was, "Do I gather from what you say that the coal sketch is not, after all, a Flaubert pastiche". Touché, Douglas.

Several years later Antony was kind enough to come to our opening night at the King's in Edinburgh. This was a very big deal for us – first time in a major theatre out of our home city – and to put the icing on the cake, he and his wife asked us back to their home for supper after the show.

"Just follow our car," he said, and as we trailed him eastwards through the dark Edinburgh streets we wondered where this mystery tour was leading. When we got to the top of Leith Walk and then took a left past Albany Street and the Cathedral Hall where we had begun nearly a decade before, the surroundings were becoming familiar; somehow it was not a surprise when a few minutes later we drew up behind Antony's car, just outside the very flat we had occupied on our second Fringe visit in 1970. By the most extraordinary coincidence it was now owned by Mr and Mrs Antony Phillips. Cue for much disbelief, laughter, reminiscence and many a glass to accompany a delicious meal, celebrate a satisfactory opening and to raise respectfully in a toast to our hosts and to serendipity.

The other professional theatres we were privileged to play during these years of S.T.W? as a hobby were The Adam Smith at Kirkcaldy, the Eden Court at Inverness, Perth Repertory Theatre, the King's, Glasgow and the Theatre Royal, Dumfries. These then became part of our regular circuit when we went full-time and the names spark off good memories, not only of the venues – the different atmosphere each had, different staff, different audiences – but also of where we stayed, what we did during the day before the performance, the friends old and new we met, where we went for supper afterwards. This was all so unlike the everyday pressures of the law office – and I enjoyed every minute of it.

We even had a rather special trip to London which didn't form part of the regular circuit. This was to the Duke of York's Theatre in St. Martin's Lane which had been hired for our visit by the London branch of the University Alumnus Association. Again, this was a hugely enjoyable venture, not least because of the meticulous organisation and warm hospitality of Ken Gorrod and Fergie Davidson[1] who had been with Buff and myself in my first Student Show, *Easter Fare,* in 1952. Fergie loyally re-appeared in later years in Edinburgh with his wife Patsy, yet another Student Show member, one of the really bonny girls in the Dancing Chorus.

And apart from the said pleasures, and the show going not too badly, it is rather nice to be able to say with mock pomposity if the occasion arises, "Ah yes, I remember when I played the West End…"

[1] Sadly, Fergie died in 1995, another good man gone far too soon.

13. Cabarets could be Hell

"Well done. That was such fun..."
— Queen Elizabeth, the Queen Mum

The discipline of doing the show in a theatre was rather different from what was required in cabaret – of which truncated sort of comedy entertainment we did quite a number during our hobby years and later also when we were full-time. They always presented special problems – what material to use and what extra writing was required, for a start, because each had to be tailored to a particular audience.

They were 'one-offs' for occasions as diverse as the Law Society of Scotland's Annual Conference and benefit nights for well-known Aberdeen footballers such as Joey Harper, Bobby Clark, Willie Miller and John McMaster and they took place in very different venues. Hotels mostly, springing from fund-raising charity events, but also kirk halls, town halls, school halls, city halls, dance halls, village halls, marquees, country houses, club houses, and even once a distillery and a boat in Aberdeen Harbour – all presenting their own challenges for James, to do with staging, lighting and sound.

And challenges for George Buff and me as performers, to do with biting our nails and pacing the floor as we waited, and waited, and waited

"Well done, young man."

for the call to go on, because in our experience no cabaret ever started on time. None. Ever. Not even nearly. Nerve-wracking. Best forgotten, most of them, but one to boast about was for the British Sailors Society charity in the Beach Ballroom in the presence of Her Majesty the Queen Mum.

That really was quite a thrill – for all of us, by which I mean the wives, too, who joined us after the performance in being presented to the gracious lady, who really did say, "Well done. That was such fun".

Not that that was all she said – her conversation was most cordial and refreshing – smarter, as the wives later recalled, than her evening gown, which looked as if it had been exhumed from a back cupboard at Birkhall and last seen at the Ghillies' Ball about 1955. And then there was a male aide hovering fussily nearby, who was also sartorially less than perfect, an ill-fitting shinyish dinner-suit looking as if it had been pinched off a refugee waiter from one of the Ballater hotels.

Of such gossipy trivialities are memorable evenings made, but the main fact remains that everybody who met her loved and admired the Queen Mum, who was the undoubted star of the evening. As she was of the

Aye, aye – fit like? PHOTO: ABERDEEN JOURNALS

whole of that particular year when she celebrated her 80th birthday, an occasion to which I will return, since the Royal connection did provide us with terrific mileage over a long period.

The other cabaret which had a seminal influence on STW? was one which we did for a company called Doric Construction in the very grand surroundings of the city's Trinity Hall at the end of the week Pope John Paul came to Scotland. He didn't get as far as Aberdeen, but my impersonation of him did. There had been blanket coverage of His Holiness's visit on the television and the strong images of his appearance and gestures, the sound of that extraordinary accent together with the topicality of the situation tempted us to let me have a go at him.

This was quite a risk, since it was the first exposure of a new and much admired character – no trial experiment – and I might have died the death. In the event, I made my entrance backwards and, on turning round, revealed a Celtic scarf (James' idea, surely). The Pope was always shown reading every word he uttered from a large sheet of foolscap, so copying him in that regard, I could not fail to be word perfect. These details contrived to save the day in the face of a script which got by, but was not wonderful.

What was wonderful, however, was the inception of a character who became a fixture in just about every show we did in the next fifteen years. His habit of reading his words permitted us to suit the script to any occasion without my having to learn it. And the scripts did get better as time went on, so that it was always a delight nearing the end of a show not to have to worry about remembering words, but simply to slip on the old scarf, stick on the papal zuchetti, grab the sheet of paper, head out backwards into the spotlight from up stage right to George's accompaniment of *Arrivaderci Roma* – then no worries, wheel round with welcoming arms outspread and milk the damn thing for all it was worth.

14. Sandy Thomson, Auchterturra and The Oldmeldrum Sports

"Hullo, is that Buckingham Palace? Who's speaking please?
Oh, very nice – is yer Mummy in?
Oh she's hooverin' is she? I wondered fit that noise wis.
I thocht she was maybe ha'in' a fly-past."
— Sandy Thomson makes a royal phone call

There were several phone calls, including one to the Queen of which this quotation is the beginning. But back to the very first which marked the introduction of Doric to the STW? programme. This was on our second visit to HMT in November 1973 and the phone call was made by Sandy Thomson, manager of the Clydesdale (formerly the old North Bank) at Auchterturra, which is to Rhynie as Rhynie is to Aberdeen.

The number began life as part of an after-dinner speech addressed to the local Institute of Bank Managers, not really the sort of respectable task that might be expected to come the way of a pretty junior and unimportant member of the legal trade, but the chairman that year who had invited me to take on the job was an early fan of STW? and therefore by definition rather a maverick as a bank manager.[1] So there I was, having vaingloriously agreed to propose the main toast of the evening, scratching my head desperately in search of inspiration a couple of nights beforehand, when it occurred to me that decimalisation and the Common Market were upon us and that these must have interesting implications for the audience of bankers – including the country chaps, some of whom would have come in from the back of beyond.

What then might Sandy Thomson at Auchterturra be saying to Heinrich Schmidt over in Munchen Gladbach about the effect of decimalisation on the local economy of neeps and tatties? Well, as first conceived for the purposes of the speech, his message took the form of a letter and when I was able to report to Buff that that seemed to go down reasonably well at the dinner, we saw its theatrical potential and adapted it to the more naturalistic phone call first performed in our 1973 show. There were two bonuses from 'The Banker', the first being the use of the telephone, a technique we pinched from the great Bob Newhart (or was it that other great American comedian Shelley Berman?) and which was to prove such a useful device in many of our shows.[2] And the second bonus was the invention of our mythical village of Auchterturra which was to

"Div ye like the Auchterturra waistcoat?"

prove such fertile territory for us. We even built the new show of 1986-87 around it.

Coming on to stage for the first time, I say to Buff and George: "Here

---

[1] His name was Bill Munnoch, long, long departed, but in his time he was larger than life – not physically because he was dapper and trim (even when kilted which he frequently was) but in style. His quirkily positive attitude was exemplified by having attempted Kilimanjaro for charity, accompanied by his wife Senga who died only recently, well into her nineties. I attended her funeral and was well pleased to be able to tell the son and daughter of the marriage – good people whom I had never met before – of the influence that their father had had on STW?

[2] Of course maybe they pinched the idea from an English Music Hall and wireless comedienne called Mrs Feather, donkey's years before that. There's nothing new under the sun – especially in comedy.

boys – d'ye like my Auchterturra waistcoat?" as I reveal an alarmingly checked extravagance beneath my dinner jacket. And Buff asks:

"Far is this Auchterturra?"

"Well ye ken Methlick?"

"Aye."

"Maud,Torphins, New Pitsligo?"

"Aye."

"Fyvie, Udny, Rhynie, Fogie?"

"Aye."

"Weel, it is neen o' them – but it could be ony o' them – and afore the nicht's oot we'll be ga'in' back an' fore til't a puckly times, because there is aye things ga'in' on in Auchterturra."

"Oh, aye – and how <u>are</u> things in Auchterturra…?"

At which George who has been tinkling contemplatively at the piano, lights up.

"That's it," he says.

"That's fit?"

"That's the tune I have been trying to remember…"

And then he plays and sings and Buff and I join in…

"How are things in Auchterturra,
that metropolis oot past Strathdon,
A'body has been there files,
It's a puckly miles,
Past the back o' beyond."

So Sandy Thomson and Auchterurra were born, but Sandy didn't remain long at the bank there, having got the sack for keeping futrets in the night safe. How he got the job of Convenor of the Oldmeldrum Sports or the one after that as Manager of the Toy Shop, Ballater, will remain forever a mystery, but got them both he did and was able to exploit such prestigious employment by making telephonic contact with successively Her Majesty the Queen, the Queen Mother and the Princess of Wales. The relationship with the Queen was particularly beneficial to STW? since it resulted in an invitation to open the Oldmeldrum Sports.

"The third Saturday of June – always." That's what it said at the bottom of the card and we felt honoured to follow in the footsteps of such celebrities of the day as the Dimblebys, Richard and David, Jimmy Saville, Bobby Charlton and Diana Dors. The advantage we had over all of these

Sorry, Alec, ye should've kent – yer bonnet and dungers is nae allowed inside the Glaikit Stirk.
PHOTO: ABERDEEN JOURNALS

names was not only that the phone call to the Queen had given the Oldmeldrum Sports a decent bit of free publicity, but also that we were dead cheap. In fact we were free (and rightly so since we gained as much from the publicity during a summer season as did the Meldrum lads) unless you count a boozy lunch at the Meldrum House Hotel in the company of the late Sir Maitland Mackie and others among the local great and good, and later a superlative afternoon tea in the officials' huttie.

In between these enjoyable episodes we had been decanted into a horse-drawn gig and paraded in style through the village and round the sports field, smiling and waving dutifully to smallish knots of spectators who seemed about as enthusiastic as the crowd at Pittodrie when Aberdeen are struggling towards a dreary draw. Any excitement was entirely physiological and took place on Buff's face, more precisely around his eyes.

"I think I must be allergic to horses," he muttered as we dismounted from the open carriage and, sure enough, after a mile or two in the slipstream of Oldmeldrum's answer to Red Rum, his eyes were streaming, closed and alarmingly swollen; he was a sight quite horrid to behold, a view shared by the little girl chosen to make a presentation to us. She took one look at him, burst into tears and ran screaming back to her mother. Not everyone reacted quite so dramatically, but we had no difficulty making our way to the tea pavilion, the crowds melting away at the approach of the loathsome monster, just as did the monster's discomfort and embarrassment at the sight of the superlative afternoon tea.

15. His Majesty's Theatre, Prince Charles and the Gala Re-opening

"Can I speak to the Princess of Wales, please?"

The wonderful Diana, married to Prince Charles in great pomp and circumstance the previous year, was the continuing centre of media attention and already the mother of the infant William when we had the idea for this phone call in the summer of 1982. It seemed the natural follow-up to the Queen and the Queen Mum phone calls and there was the hint of a possibility that its first public performance just might take place in the glamorous presence of the Princess herself.

No doubt she had been invited, but could not make it because of maternal duties, but Prince Charles – despite some confusion, not to say hostility between local authority and local charity – did miraculously consent to attend the late re-opening of HMT in September 1982 after a massive face-lift which had taken more than two years and several million pounds to complete (HMT's not HRH!).[1]

Judging by the press coverage Diana missed quite a good night out. "Glittering," "sparkling," "splendid" said the *Press & Journal* next day. "Scintillating," "glorious," "superb," said *The Scotsman*, either of the occasion or the theatre itself. Although the show did not quite measure up to such superlatives, it was a brave attempt by James Donald as HMT Director to reconcile conflicting interests – to please as wide an audience as possible and to make use of the new technical facilities under battle conditions. *Curtain Up* was the name of the production and it was a sort of high-class variety headed up distinctively, however, by the Scottish Ballet, the whole melange supervised by their director Peter Darrell. And how hard they worked, these young dancers. We were full of admiration for their enthusiasm and their utter dedication to their art. By way of contrast, those members of the orchestra we came across were much more relaxed and none more so in a cheerful, friendly way than the conductor Bramwell Tovey, who seemed fascinated by the strange variation of the English language which was part of our stock-in-trade as represented by the Ballater Toy Shop phone-call.

Our fellow performers were similarly intrigued and not just by the dialect. After all we were only local and still basically amateurs. They were all hardened professionals, a long time in the business – and though the substance of their acts is now lost to me in the mists of time, their personalities off-stage left something of an impression on this impressionable observer. I thought that Janet Brown, comedienne and Mrs Thatcher impersonator, was a charming lady who seemed to be smiling all the time; Bill McCue (who died in 1999) was a much loved, much respected bass baritone and Motherwell FC supporter, an all-round good guy who swore all the time, usually at Motherwell FC; Roger de Courcy, ventriloquist and master of Nooky Bear, was a grumpy old man (and not that old) before the phrase had ever been invented and seemed to be

---

[1] More than three million, in fact, and certainly more than enough for eyebrows to be raised by sceptical patrons who wondered how and where all that money had been spent. Sure there had been a lot of painting and papering, but what else? The truth was that most of the work was structural and technical – not to be seen – but the answer they got if they came to our Christmas show three months later was rather different, since by that time Buff and George had produced a song identifying to wicked effect the possible outlays. *That's far a' the money went* was the title and repeated refrain, and the final item of expenditure was "…and a new three-piece suite for Jimmy Donald's front room." What a damned cheek that was, looking back, but also an indication not just of how comfortable was the relationship which had developed between James Donald as Director of HMT and ourselves, but even more so of how very tolerant Jimmy was.

After-show introduction to H.R.H.

moaning all the time, often about the audience whom he described as "a
… fire 'azard out there". No doubt he was kind at heart, but if you were
to get Nooky on his own I guarantee he wouldn't say a thing, but would
respond with a negative, glassy kind of look. Then there was Ward Allen
& Roger the Dog, another ventriloquist act, friendly this time from "oop
North" somewhere, who replaced Roger de Courcy – or was it the other
way round? Anyway it was a case of one Roger being exchanged for
another, or a spaniel being exchanged for a rottweiler.

I almost forgot to mention Richard Baker, sometime News presenter,
man of culture and friend of Haddo Arts, who introduced the show on its
Gala first night and finally the top of the bill, Patty Boulaye, a glamorous
gal who sang and danced a bit. She must have been flavour of the month
at the time (or maybe flavour of a month or two previous) because she

had her own manager who was very protective of her in the sense that he seemed to keep her apart from the rest of the cast, tucked away in her dressing-room. He was probably her husband and they settled down to a life of happy domesticity, because we never heard of her again. However, if the show signalled a move towards her retirement, it marked for us an important step towards full-time professional show business. That rather grand show in which we appeared with real pros validated our professional credentials, proving a valuable springboard for our own show a couple of months later when we did a six-week season over Christmas and Hogmanay.

But whatever the worth of any of the professional contributions to the show, Prince Charles was undoubtedly star of the Gala Night, delivering a genuinely funny, charming speech at the end by way of a formal re-opening. This opinion may be influenced by his favourable reference to the Toy Shop phone call and his easy recall of visits with his grandmother when "the man in the toy shop spoke exactly like that". When we were introduced to him afterwards he again mentioned the accent and I was able to explain, "I go on holiday to Deeside as well as yourself, sir".

One last word about *Curtain Up*, a key event in the history of both HMT and STW?. Although Buff and I wrote the Ballater Toy Shop number and a Pope address specially for the occasion, we must also have written a piece for Buff in his own persona at the beginning of the show. Of that piece I have only one telling recollection. Buff's entrance was on a wobbly cart off which he stepped mid-stage left, after a not-too-inspiring musical item which opened the show. He was looking around the theatre balefully – the stage itself but mainly the auditorium, painstakingly refurbished at enormous cost and looking gorgeous. Long pause, then – "Nae much difference, is there?" he reflected. Quintessential Mr Hardie. Quintessential Aberdonian humour.

16. Going Full-time... Seriously

"I have given in my resignation to the Macaulay in order to go full-time."
— James Logan, December 1980

ames may have been — no, he definitely was — a bit tiddly at the time. The occasion was a party at our house just before Christmas when tongues were loosened, and none more so than James's who relished a bit of drama and gossip anyway. And it is unlikely these were his exact words — after all they were spoken a long time ago, but that was certainly the gist of them. He had been given the opportunity to take early retirement, was about to do so and was therefore the first of the four of us to be in a position to make STW? his full-time occupation.[1]

Not that that happened right away by any means — it would be another two-and-a-half years before all of us left our conventional careers, but James's decision was a kind of catalyst. In his inimitable way he had conjured up an atmosphere of exciting possibilities which we took on board in our own ways and with differing degrees of enthusiasm. The

---

[1] While waiting for the rest of us to catch up with him James found most interesting employment with Aberdeen Maritime Museum and did a terrific job raising funds for its extension and renovation.

trouble was that individually we had different circumstances to deal with before we were able to come together with James as the full-time working partners of STW?

For my part it had to be a gradual change anyway. It is just not possible for a practising solicitor, in fairness to partners and clients, to suddenly up sticks, clear the desk and walk out the door.

The sequence of events so far as I was concerned was firstly that I told my partners of my decision in September 1981, I eased out of the practice as a part-time consultant in 1982 and thereafter retained my practising certificate for another three years or so, finishing current stuff and doing the occasional bit of business from home with the essential assistance of my long-time secretary Aileen Cruickshank, who was an absolute treasure. And when eventually she was obliged for domestic reasons to give up, so did I – encouraged, would you believe, by the Secretary of the Law Society of Scotland, Ken Pritchard.

Worried about the possibility of STW? failing, of our not managing to keep up the standards to which our public had become accustomed, I wrote to Ken asking about the procedure for recovering a practising certificate after a period of absence and I received a reply which was not only surprising, but stunningly generous and optimistic. Its message was that all would be well in this change of career, that I should go forward and enjoy it with all his best wishes and he would be following STW?'s progress with enthusiastic interest. And indeed he did. The very last STW? engagement – even after our theatre tour called *Final Fling* – was a cabaret for the Law Society of Scotland Conference at Gleneagles in April 1996 and Ken was there making sure everything was right for us and joining in what turned out to be a standing ovation. ("They were just glad to see the back of us," said Buff). What an asset Ken was to the Law Society, what a credit to the legal profession, a real gentleman who further endeared himself to me because he was so highly regarded by my oldest and closest friend in the Law from student days, himself sometime President of the Law Society, Sandy McIlwain.[2]

In relation to the major decision George and Buff solved their own

[2] Sadly my old pal Sandy died in July 2008 after a long, harrowing illness. We had known each other since schooldays and at university he too had been in the Students' Show. I was honoured to speak (with difficulty) at his funeral in Glasgow Cathedral and Eva and I continue the close friendship with his widow, Moira and the family.

Our groupies tended not to be teenagers.

dilemmas, George quickly, Buff inevitably slowly but to his friends' delight was finally able to say at a heart-to-heart meeting in our house, "I'm with you, lads". Innate pessimism thus conquered the die was cast and off the three of us were setting on our yellow brick road.

Part Three

The
Full-time
Years
1983-1995

Preface

It may sound sadistic, but one of the early pleasures of plunging full-time at the age of fifty into the world of entertainment (or rather the modest parish of Scottish entertainment) was to lie in bed in the morning and listen to the sound of the cars going down our street carrying their owners to work – offices and shops and banks, or maybe an early train or plane.

"Wonderful," I would murmur to myself as I turned over, radio on by this time for *Desert Island Discs* or a touch of intellectual stimulation from Melvyn Bragg. "Been there, done that, don't care for T-shirts and I'll get up in my own good time." Which was to take a pretty leisurely approach to ablutions, breakfast and the P&J before the arrival of Mr W.D. Hardie at 11 o'clock on the dot – and quite an elongated dot it was most days. When I say "Mr Hardie" that was not, however, the address I was accustomed to using or he to responding to when the bell rang and I went to the door. The exchange – because over the years we very seldom spoke to each other as our real selves – would likely go something like this:

"God, if it is nae yersel', Norman – ye're a stranger, come in."

"No, no, Alec. I'm nae comin' in."

"Oh, come in."

"No, I'm nae comin' in."

"Oh, come in Norman. I hinna seen ye this whilie. I wis jist sayin' tae Mary at teatime, 'I hinna seen Norman this whilie'. Come in."

Dress rehearsal no problem – always black tie.   PHOTO: GORDON WRIGHT

"No, I'm nae comin' in."

"Oh, come i-i-i-in."

"Weel, a' richt – jist for a mintie…"

Or words to that effect – an exchange in the role of our two favourite Doric characters, Norman (dour and lugubrious) and Alec (bright and sparky). Or, depending on the mood of the moment we might be two different chaps altogether – Basil and Henry, a couple of Edinburgh buffers probably of a semi-retired legal background:

"Hello, Henry – how goes it? What brings you here at this time of the day? Are you all right?"

"Fine thanks, Basil. Fine. Sorry to bother you when the sun's not nearly over the yardarm, but Ethel's got her morning bridge lot coming and all hell's let loose at home, what with Stanley throwing up on the drawing-room carpet as well."

"Stanley? Who's Stanley?"

"Oh, didn't I tell you? We've got a new lab puppy."

"Of course, of course. These things are sent to try us. Come in, my dear chap. I'm sure Dottie can conjure up a mug of Nescafé and a digestive biscuit to soothe the savaged breast."

And on such a note on the doorstep enter then Buff ready for his coffee and biscuits and a hard couple of hours on the script. And other things too, of course… a chat about local news items from the P&J, national news from the *Scotsman* (or if our session was in the afternoon at Buff's house, the *Evening Express* and *The Guardian* over a cup of tea and a Tunnock's chocolate marshmallow), a gossip about the latest scandal concerning a neighbour, a peek even through the blinds and a hostile stare at that very neighbour as he padded his unknowing way down the pavement. "Miserable old bugger," I used to hiss, as well as giving vent to an uncompromising gesture. Anything to stave off the evil moment when we would have to put funny (or not) pen to paper.

Such was the pattern of our working day during a writing phase – with the occasional interruption from James. "Good morning lads," he would announce brightly and his arrival always brought with it, for myself anyway, a wee buzz of anticipation.

"I bring you nothing but good news. The Box Office at the Adam Smith has opened and there has already been a flurry of activity – three seats sold in the first forty-eight hours." (Groans from Buff and me.) "And also," he would proceed cheerfully, "Warehouse and Dispatch have taken delivery only this morning of our new cassette – STW? *Number Seven*". (Originality always was a strong point in the naming and marketing of our recorded material.)

Now an explanation of these references is perhaps in order. The Adam Smith is a very nice theatre in Kirkcaldy, a regular venue every couple of years, and Warehouse and Dispatch was the administrative title conferred on themselves by Graham our Business Manager and Anne, James's wife, from whose attic, spare bedroom, garage, garden shed – I never learned, such matters being beyond the understanding of us artistes – our records and cassettes were warehoused, stored and dispatched. The cassettes and LPs were a useful earner in the widening range of activities in which we were involved when we went full-time. Over the years we became, if not a cottage industry, at least a wee croftie kind of business – and a family one at that.

It may be of passing interest to describe the genesis of the songs and sketches which resulted from our work, and the story behind them. Since they run into hundreds, a couple of dozen will have to do; an appropriate number, because that was what made up an STW? show,[1] or, to use an old-fashioned name, revue, which the dictionary defines as: "A form of entertainment which is the enactment of events by imitation of their salient features and chief actors; also, loosely, a medley of songs, sketches, dances etc.".

Well, I cannot promise any dancing, but imagining that I have been invited to make up a two-hour revue, a mixter-maxter of stuff that might appeal to an audience, here is a sample list chosen at random.

[1] If you are familiar with STW? – and the probability is that you are if you are reading this book (but if not, and you are puzzled by all these stories of mine – or comments or explanations or whatever) I suggest you consult (acquiring, if need be, by borrowing or theft) one of our books, videos, tapes or CDs in order to read, see or hear what it was that began life on that damned sheet of blank paper.

17. A Review of the Revue[1] called STW?

And Here's the First Half – Twelve Numbers Chosen at Random.

Opening Chat
See the beginning of Chapter 4.

Scotland's Glens

This song was performed by George more often probably than any other in the repertoire, because it catches the spirit of STW? so brilliantly. For three years or so during the early Seventies Buff was posted to Banff as part of his Hospital Board duties and lived there on his own during the week, coming back to Aberdeen, to Margaret and the children at the weekend.

Although he never shared Billy Connolly's view of the town, based on an adverse audience reaction on a one-night stand, (Banff – "a muffled explosion of a place") he was always happy to get home on a Friday evening. During one of these drives home, the idea for *The Glens* came

---

[1] It was always a source of amusement and mild irritation when journalists and critics – even quite knowledgeable ones – referred to what we were doing as "a review". No. It was what they were doing which was a review.

to him. Not only that, the couplets of the verses were coming thick and fast as he negotiated the Haudagain traffic and as soon as he got in his own front door he only had time for a, "Sorry Margaret. Can't wait," before he dashed upstairs to his study to get the words down on paper before they escaped his mind.

"He was in such a hurry," said Margaret, "I thought he was desperate for the loo."

Buff's intention was that no Glen should be mentioned more than once in the song. That was how the lyric was written, but there are so many Glens that George learned just the first few, of which there was always a Glenfiddich – in fact some nights there would be a double, or even triple Glenfiddich – and in addition to a few other standards, there was the occasional appearance of an interesting blend like Glenfidlet or Glenlochles.

So it continued for more than thirty years, despite the odd complaint from a slightly miffed lyricist, until one night George got the last laugh. I think it happened at the nice little theatre in Aboyne when I was involved briefly with the Festival there and had persuaded the pair of them to do a show devoted solely to the music and lyrics of STW? Anyway when the *Glens* was mentioned, dear George, a twinkle in the eye, proceeded to give a flawless performance, including every single Glen featured in the original version with one or two thrown in for good measure. Buff was happily gobsmacked.

Actually that Banff period was quite a productive one for the pair of us. I went up several times in my pride and joy, a little grey MGB GT, and stayed the night in Buff's wee flat. Over a dram or three we worked on such pieces as *The Will* and *Oldmeldrum Sports,* which were to do well.

The Sleeper

The idea for this sketch came when I was going to London in the train overnight with my schoolboy son, Stephen, on a visit to Lords. Talented sportsman though he was, he'd been selected, not to play but to get the benefit of some junior coaching. Anyway, I could not help overhearing through the thin dividing wall between compartments, the muffled voices of the adjacent male occupants.

After Buff and I had written the script we doubted whether it would be worth doing, because a double bunk would have to be built[2] on which we would have to repose horizontally, our talking heads however, positioned vertically – more or less – in order to be seen and heard by the audience. Having decided to take the risk we exposed The Sleeper for a first try-out at Perth Repertory Theatre as part of the local Arts Festival.

It was a triumph, and I say that with confidence, not because I remember actually performing it, but because after we had done so we, in the blackout, slipped off the bunks into the wings, Buff to one side and I to the other. Arriving at the back of the stage before exiting to the dressing-rooms, we caught sight of each other in the dim light and simultaneously, two minds with but a single thought, we gave a silent thumbs-up to each other. Silent, but gleeful.

I can see Buff in profile yet. We knew we had cracked it – first time. And that's an image and a memory I will always treasure.

There's a recent sequel to The Sleeper's associations. A university contemporary of Buff's (whom I got to know a little because he was quite a fan of STW?) retired to his home town of Montrose after a career in academia and took to journalism and broadcasting like a duck to water. The journalism was, I think, weekly and local but Denis Rice's broadcasting is frequent and national because as a philosopher, blessed with a beautiful speaking voice, he is a natural for such programmes as Radio Four's Thought For The Day and early in 2009 used our Sleeper sketch as the trigger for a serious piece with a moral and religious message. Thank you, Denis, for your support and for remembering us – and we're fans of yours, too.

The Mossat Shop

The building still exists in deepest Strathdon occupied now by other businesses, but the institution known as The Mossat Shop has long gone. In fact it may well have been gone when Buff wrote the piece, but then, being a resolute urbanite, he's not the quickest at keeping up with country matters. Which shows in a way, since even Buff knew about it, how famous the Mossat Shop was in its day – famous for stocking just about anything – every article and commodity known to man and more besides.

---

[2] This would almost certainly have been done by Anne's Dad, Mr Duncan Brand, an unsung hero of STW?'s backstage world. His son-in-law could always rely on him to help in a practical way.

The song is a parody of the signature tune of that rather less local institution, *The Muppet Show*, hugely popular in the Seventies – and it represents Mr Hardie at his best, not just for the idea, but for the cleverness of the words. Wit, charm, humour abound in every syllable of every joyous rhyme. Just one problem. What a devil it was to learn – and to perform!

The Moderator

The origins of this character whom I portrayed in three of our scripts in the show[3] lie in the Law rather than the Church. In private practice these days, when early advancement is the norm, it is practically unknown for a solicitor not to have secured a partnership or struck out on his own before he starts shaving (or so it seems to me), but it was not always so. In the mid-Fifties, when I was an apprentice in a small brown office in Belmont Street, Aberdeen, I shared a room with the firm's assistant who had been qualified for nearly twenty years.

Admittedly that was unusual even for these days, but then Royston John Milne M.A. LLB. Advocate in Aberdeen, sometime naval officer, occasional poet, habitual procrastinator, was a most unusual chap, and I am glad to have the opportunity to say something about him to add to the diary reference in Chapter 3. It was sheer chance that we found ourselves together in the office of D.M.C.Donald & Co., Advocates in Aberdeen, but it quickly emerged that we had a shared interest in the Aberdeen University Students' Show.

Roy had been co-author of a couple of the Shows in the Thirties and if I had not been so immersed in them in the Fifties, I wouldn't be writing this now. I may not have learned much about legal practice from Roy, but sitting across the desk from him I was the beneficiary of a much wider education. He had a feeling for language and a wonderful sense of humour, both of which he displayed to the amusement and delight of his callow apprentice. He also had a wondrous appetite for cigarettes, cold tea and chocolate peppermint creams.

As well as the tales of wartime – he had been on Arctic convoys as well as landing up in Australia – he revelled in the characters of his youth and

---

[3] Other Church of Scotland minister appearances:
The Christening
At The Assembly.

student days, one of whom he regaled me with frequently. This was an old lawyer, senior partner of one of the stuffier firms, part-time lecturer at the university and possessor of a voice of comic perfection. It was pompous, it was adenoidal, it was smug, it was unique and unforgettable and a gift to Roy, whose use of it resonated in my mind.

"Now young Shawcross," he would address me over his ancient spectacles as he dragged on his Goldflake, "let us lend our forensic skills to this very difficult case which we have coming up tomorrow in the Police Court, concerning a defective tail-light on a Corporation bus. From your insightful, albeit lengthy precognition of the driver, I have come to the conclusion that the man is a psychopath. I am therefore considering a plea of guilty but insane. What think you, my learned friend?"

By this time the utterance had been driven back by the inhalation of the noxious weed to his very boots, and it was this smoke-stained growl which came to mind umpteen years later when Buff and I were writing the monologue for the Moderator at Crathie Kirk, the idea for which had been sparked off by the experience of a minister friend who had been invited to preach there.

Now that seemed a fusion of character and situation with much potential, and even more if we promoted the minister to Moderator; which we did – a rise in the world which fired him with a life and a voice of his own, in which the original gritty susurrus might also be enlivened by private cackles and whoops of hedonistic pleasure.

This is, of course, the key to the character. The simple man of God loves the flesh-pots, which in his case are also simple. Nothing sophisticated for him; he grasps the opportunity to indulge his healthy appetite for food and drink and the basic creature comforts, and to their great credit it is the members of the Clergy themselves who have been the first to spot this irony. Many of them have been generous in their approval of this sketch and the ultimate accolade was when we were invited to perform it at an official reception for the real Moderator of the day, who, whatever his true feelings, gave every outward indication that he was enjoying it.

That is called style and it was matched by our minister friend referred to earlier, whose invitation to Balmoral and Crathie sparked off the idea for the sketch. Let's call him Bill, because that happened to be his name – and a lovely man he was, with the canniest sense of humour – and pass on to one of the stories which involved Her Majesty's Daimler.

"My dear friends..."

This particular Sunday the grand limousine was to convey Bill to Crathie Kirk first, and then return to Balmoral for the Queen and whomsoever else in the house party wished to attend. The start of the journey took the car past the kennels at the back where the Queen was feeding her beloved Corgis. She looked up and as Bill glided past in chauffered splendour he gave her a smile and then yielded to the urge to raise his arm and to wave – graciously, you might even say majestically.

Now that also is called style.

Mounthooly

One afternoon, early in 1984, I was on my way over to Buff's for a working session and happened to hear on the car radio, Ella Fitzgerald singing *Manhattan*, the first hit song written by Richard Rodgers and Lorenz Hart which celebrated Hart's beloved New York, and was filled with those outrageous internal rhymes which were the hallmark of his work.

Surely, I thought, Buff would respond to the challenge of emulating his lyricist hero by doing a similar job on his beloved Aberdeen. I was right. Buff liked the idea, enjoyed writing it up and so *Mounthooly*, which had the merit of scansion for a parody rather than attractiveness as a local area, was born. The song formed part of an 'envelope' of four items in the show, all relating to house purchase (the others being *Building Societies*, *Buying a House* and *Rentokil*) and when we moved away from home to Glasgow and Edinburgh and wanted to preserve the envelope intact, second and third versions had to be written. These emerged as *Argyle Street* and *Corstorphine*, both of which shared the distinction of having the same scansion as *Manhattan*.

George was less enthusiastic about learning the words than Buff was about writing them. But he did, and all three versions rolled around in his head like, in his own words, "three sarks in a tumble-drier". Fortunately the colours never ran, and the dreaded nightmare of Lothian Road appearing in juxtaposition with Bearsden or Devanha Gardens did not occur.

Edinburgh Castle

One of the bonuses of STW? when we were doing it as a hobby was that it gradually began to earn rather more than beer-money. Having started off sleeping on the floor when we first went to the Edinburgh Fringe in 1969, we had moved sufficiently up-market by 1980 to check in to the Caledonian Hotel when we were playing the King's Theatre. The point, we felt, was that hobbies were to be enjoyed and that as long as our share of the box office was enough to cover our expenses, we would enjoy not only performing the show in the evening, but also a rather good holiday lifestyle. After all, we had taken a week or two off work to have this kind of vacation.

On such occasions Business Manager Graham would pop down from Aberdeen for a day or two to make sure we were behaving ourselves, and it was over breakfast in the Caley one morning, that he remarked looking out the window – over and up to Auld Reekie's signature landmark – "I wonder if they got planning permission for that castle".

"Great idea for a sketch," said Buff immediately, and startled out of finishing my cornflakes, I could not disagree. Before we could write it, however, some historical research was required, which involved a visit to the great fortification for the first time for thirty years or more.

What we learned – and not many people who aren't natural historians know this – is that there is not a precise point at which it is certain the foundation stone of Edinburgh Castle was laid; as opposed to the foundation stone, say, of a municipal gasworks in Portobello. One royal name did come up a few times, however; that of Malcolm who became the victim of the sort of comic licence which Buff and I are quick to invoke in defence of our many historical and other solicisms.

Sweet Song

If you were to look at an old programme of a West-End revue of the Fifties which was one of the formative influences on STW?, you would have difficulty working out what many of the items were about – even though you'd seen and thoroughly enjoyed the show. I can think of such huge successes as Joyce Grenfell's *Penny Plain*, or *Pieces of Eight*, or even Flanders & Swann's *At the Drop of a Hat* in which a song about a London bus was entitled *Transport of Delight*.

Puns and cleverness abounded and we vowed at an early stage that such tweeness was not for us. Clarity, we argued, was much to be preferred to urbane obscurity, not only by us, but also by a puzzled audience trying to work out afterwards the numbers they had seen from the programme titles.

Oh yes, and there maybe was another reason for simplicity. Sloth. It was a bind and a bother thinking up stuff a lot of the audience probably wouldn't get round to reading.

However, this number had to be one exception to the rule. The name *Rowntree* could not be spelled out in the programme without giving away the joke. And an excellent joke it was, too. Buff's, of course, the words being a parody of Lady Nairn's gentle ballad which George performed immaculately. He even mastered a verse added much later, which points up a bit of social history, because in 1995 the Rowntree factory in Edinburgh was threatened with closure, prompting the following:

> But Rowntree, O Rowntree,
> Here ends my love affair with thee,
> For it is roon the toon
> That ye're closin' doon
> Yer Edinburgh factory.
> It's wrong that you've
> Proposed this move,
> Which we in Scotland don't approve,
> So I make this call —
> Good Scots folk all
> Cut doon yer Rowntree.
> Doon, doon wi' Rowntree."

Trans-Buchan Airways

Out of the blue there arrived in the post one day in 1988 a script from our great friend and supporter Jack Webster. As we were happy to acknowledge in any subsequent programme, the idea for this number was certainly Jack's — and was so good that it immediately induced not only a pang of envy (always a sign of quality in my experience), but also the urge to write up the fantasy in a different way. This was a good example perhaps of the difference between the journalist's treatment of a subject and the comedy scriptwriter's, and the comedy scriptwriters in this case were delighted when Jack, kind and generous as ever, agreed to let us loose on his precious notion in our own way.

And after we had completed the writing I found the piece a joy to perform. But scary. This is as good a point as any to refer to stage-fright, a condition described by Jonathan Miller as "...more than mere forgetfulness ... the terror of a moment of standing outside (one)self and seeing (one)self suspended in the night sky of a theatrical performance, illuminated by all those lights, watched by dimly visible faces — and frozen... a horrible experience".

According to Miller, who appears to have had a few moments of terror in his own stage career, notably with *Beyond the Fringe*, this is not an unusual phenomenon, particularly among older actors. Even the great Laurence Olivier suffered, going through a period of several years when, during a performance, as Miller explains, "He had these moments of appalling, shattering lapses in which he forgot his words and the earth stood still". Olivier himself in his 1982 autobiography confesses to the human condition, the misery of a thespian god, which he was able somehow to endure and from which he finally escaped only with the help and practical support of his fellow actors whom he had to request never to make eye contact with him when playing a scene, nor ever to leave him entirely alone on stage, even when he was delivering a long speech or soliloquy, lest the emergence of a sudden dry would require an *ad hoc* intervention.

To all of which an absurdly lowly yours truly can only say, in the words of the Buchan Pilot, or Sandy Thomson permanently on the telephone, or a sermonising Moderator, "God Almichty! I ken foo he felt…I ken fit he meant".

The stage-fright of which Olivier wrote, however, and which I immediately recognise has a different name in my vocabulary. I used to call it a 'hairy moment', but in retrospect it is more accurate to say that it is stage-fright which causes the hairy moment – or moments – which struck only during a solo item.

Not so long ago at a charity dinner in Kirriemuir I happened to be sitting next to the kenspeckle Jim Brown, Grain Merchant of Fettercairn, who is President of the Highland Games Association and therefore never off the top of the road. As we swopped reminiscences, Jim – the best of sorts – was courteous enough to ask what were my own favourite pieces from STW?

My reply was simple: anything that isn't a solo, because, as I confessed a while back, solos are scary. The whole thing can go wrong so easily, what with those hairy moments liable, like lightning, to strike without warning. And I'll say more about solos under Hotline soon to follow.

The Auchterturra band

This was James's idea. Or rather his idea was *any* Scottish Country Dance Band which fitted naturally into the Auchterturra theme. He liked the picture of his colleagues as three cheap and cheery, not to say slightly dodgy musicians, still hoping for their first big break on Robbie Shepherd's radio programme, but uncertain what to do with a BBC cheque in the black economy. Problem was that the only musician was George, Buff and I not having a note between us. However, we mimed away happily on broken-down, borrowed accordion and fiddle while George on piano bore the musical weight of backing Buff's parodies. The Donald-Hardie-Logan combination resulted in a wonderfully funny number – George's breakneck rendition of the superbly witty words to an Eightsome Reel, the *Deil amang the Tailors,* being a particular highlight. As for me, it was a delight just to coast along and pick up the odd chortle out of many big laughs. Nothing scary here at all.

Hotline

"Hullo? Is that Washington D.C. Is that you Mr President?"

After his calls to the Queen and Princess Di, I thought our hero Sandy Thomson[4] should be allowed to shuffle off his telephone coil, but Buff thought differently, and offered Reagan and Brezhnev as subjects. That was some time early in 1984 when we were writing the new summer show for HMT and somehow, despite my reluctance, the funny lines started coming to us, and there Buff sat, jotting them down between swigs of whisky and whiffs of his puffer.

When we had finished the writing I found it none too easy to learn, particularly the complicated bits where Sandy switched from Reagan to Brehznev and back again. Then when Brezhnev died and the Russian people went into mourning, they did so with no less feeling than I did, since it entailed the alarming business of working the same lines, but with a different name. After that, Secretaries General of the USSR seemed to go down like flies, apparently cursed by Sandy Thomson's telephone conversations with them. Mr Gorbachev, the last incumbent of the post

---

[4] The complete list of Sandy Thomson's phone calls and appearances were as follows:

The Banker

Oldmeldrum Sports

The Toy Shop Ballater

Hotline

Auchterturra Election

We are the band – and only George can play a note.

PHOTO: GORDON WRIGHT

before the Berlin Wall came down, might have thanked his lucky stars that this phone call went out of our repertoire.

Going back to Mr Brezhnev's time, however, when the number was newly minted it was in reasonable enough shape to be given its first tryout when we had a three-night visit to Pitlochry. The Festival Theatre is a most pleasing venue, backstage and front, and if it had not been for the fact that we were trying out a few other new numbers, too, we would have been very relaxed and better able to appreciate the surroundings.

I managed to stumble through with only a few hairy moments and as I write these words they spark off other thoughts. Actually, I was sitting at a table at the side of the stage, because I thought we should try to make the number look different from its predecessors, in which I stood centre mike nursing the old telephone. However, the table and chair didn't really work. I felt uncomfortable, even less in command of the situation than usual, and James quite rightly hauled me back into a standing position centre stage.

Of course, a hairy moment is not a moment at all. It lasts an eternity, and is caused by that phantom fiend of the theatre, stage-fright, the cerebral gremlin that lays asunder the thought processes and threatens complete amnesia. Hairy moments are horrendous and derive from the difficulty of keeping the different parts of the mind in the correct balance. Accompany me, if you will, through a dramatised extract from Hotline.

Believe me, if you can, that the mind has four parts. I don't know what they are called anatomically, but they all have a life of their own and in order to describe what they do, I will give them names. Let's call the first one Sandy since Sandy Thomson is the character I am playing and the audience has to believe in him. Sandy should be word perfect and the way he gets word perfect is by memorising the lines, parrot fashion if necessary, so that they are delivered without fluff or hesitation which are fatal to the confidence and enjoyment of an audience.

The second part I'll call Charlie. He's the guy in charge of the muscles and physical movement. He is a bit thick and slow on the uptake.

Number three is Jimmy who is a sensitive chap. Most of his senses are directed either at the audience or the wings off-stage, although they occasionally waft away from his immediate surroundings to external concerns.

Number four is Cormack. He is captain of the team and if anything goes wrong he is supposed to take charge and restore order. The operative phrase is "supposed to". Captain Cormack is in reality a dithering fool. I have called him Cormack because that was my mother's maiden name and it is considered quite smart in some theatrical circles to use your mother's name for stage purposes, presumably in order to validate the kind of language commonly thrown at you.

The action begins in the wings as the applause is dying from a song by George, and Sandy's are the only words the audience hears. All the rest are silent.

Charlie: Okay legs, off you go, make for the mike. Eyes concentrate hard on the darkness, don't let the legs go too far. Fingers dial the number on the phone.

Sandy (humming the *Star-Spangled Banner*): De, de, de, de, de. De, de, de, de. Hullo, is that Washington DC. Is that you Mr President? Is it nae? Fit's that, it is the exchange at Rhynie? Is that you Beldie? But I have jist deen international direct dialling richt through tae Washington. Fit wye did I nae get through. Ye've teen the plug oot o' the satellite?

Jimmy: Quite a big laugh from the audience there, Sandy – a good omen for the rest of the number.

Sandy: Tae bile the kettle for yer coffee?

Jimmy: Another big laugh, Sandy. A solid audience tonight. You should get through this okay. Jist relax – you might even be able to go on automatic pilot.

Sandy: Well, wid ye hurry up, wid ye put me through – Washington DC 4840. God, fit a vratch she is that Beldie…(the performance drones on while Jimmy continues to put his oar in).

Jimmy: A nice big house, too. A lot of bald heads and white heads and blue rinses. Just our sort of audience.[5] Some younger people too, though. Oh, oh. Nice pair of shoes in the front row there on the right. Nice dress too. Pull it down over your knees dear – that's disturbing. God, there is a hysterical cackler halfway up the stalls on the left. Don't be so antisocial – it is not as funny as all that – people will think you're a plant. That exit light at the back of the stalls throws a strange light on the glass of the door, doesn't it? No, it is not the glass of the door, it is the usherette's torch. What is that usherette looking at and why? There goes the cackler again drawing attention to herself, so distracting. Wonder where we should go for a bite to eat after the show. What's that noise from the wings? James talking on the phone to someone. There's something wrong? Is there a problem? The mike is just a bit low. Is it working? There's the cackler, yet again. Maybe she's laughing at me because I am not being heard properly.

Charlie: Here's the tricky bit of business coming up where the phone is changed from one hand to another – get ready.

Sandy: Haud on Ronnie, there seems to be another voice comin' on the line. Haud on a mintie…

Charlie: Take your right hand out of your pocket. Transfer the phone

---

[5] "Our sort of audience" at Pitlochry reminds me of the night there when we had barely begun the show before being aware of what we thought were teething troubles with a sound system which had just been installed. Was that the reason for the series of high-pitched whistling noises in the first few minutes? "Oh no," said the resident stage manager, "that's just everybody switching on their hearing aids". Right enough. As we took turns to look through the peephole in the side curtain – a magnet for the performer of masochistic tendencies – we scanned a sea of elderly respectability, glinting spectacles, blue rinses and balding pates. Our sort of audience right enough…

from the left hand to the right and keep talking.

Jimmy: This is ridiculous. Stupid. This is no way to suspend audience disbelief. No wonder that mad woman is cackling and the rest of the audience are restless.

Sandy: Hullo, fa's that. Mr Brezhnev, Mr Brezhnev? Div you understand fit I'm sayin'? Fit's that?

Jimmy: This is awful. No-one could believe this rubbish. What am I doing standing here making an idiot of myself? I used to have a sensible job, a position of respect in a community far away from this place full of hostile strangers...

Sandy: Fit's that? Oh, aye, jist...fairly...mercy aye.

Cormack: Good grief, Sandy, you're losing the place. Sorry, I had not noticed before, just dozing off. What have you done to him, Jimmy? He's forgotten his lines. Any second now and he'll be either talking a lot of drivel or he'll dry completely. Look at him already, his eyes are glazed, there is cold sweat on his brow, his hands are shaking, the fellow's turning to jelly. Get a grip, man. Go back a sentence quickly and take another run at what you're trying to remember.

Sandy: Fit's 'at? Oh ye div, an' ye're tryin' tae get through tae President Reagan on the hot line. It's important? Are ye gaun' tae be on for lang, because if ye are ye'd be better waitin' till efter six o'clock tae get the cheap rate...

Cormack: That's it, that's better. Now Charlie, control these quivering legs and get through this thing.

Charlie: Right captain.

Cormack: And Sandy, get going, get through the number as quickly as you can.

Sandy: This is the night ye dee Fix the Ba' in Pravda? Well, but I'll fairly pass on the message tae Ronnie for ye...(Sandy whines on as rapidly as sense and articulation will allow).

Cormack: Good, keep going, Sandy. Speak so loudly and quickly that you drown out any further interruptions. And Jimmy, let's not have any further interruptions from you, for God's sake...

Jimmy: Okay, okay. I can still hear that woman cackling, though. She must be paranoid or something.

The rustic Sandy Thomson without telephone, but in the company of two City gentlemen. PHOTO: ABERDEEN JOURNALS

Cinemas

This song was prompted by the closure of the Majestic, one of the major cinemas in Aberdeen. All the other cinemas mentioned in the song had already shut down, but the end of the Majestic, an imposing, granite-fronted building on a prime Union Street site somehow marked also the end of an era. Owned by the Donald family, designed by Tommy Scott Sutherland, architect and entrepreneur extraordinaire, it had been such a part of the city's social fabric that it merited inclusion on one of the supporters' banners that accompanied the Dons to their destiny: Gothenberg in May 1983. "Strachan gives more Majestic passes than Dick Donald" was the proud announcement, at once praising the gifted midfielder and cheekily underlining the fans' knowledge of the club chairman's generosity. Placed judiciously between a couple of broad speakies[6] the number worked beautifully, its appeal lying in the witty nostalgia of familiar places passing into history and a most sympathetic performance by George.

[6] A 'speakie' was simply our slang for any item which was spoken, not played or sung.

Interval

If you were in a theatre seeing the show you'd now have an ice-cream or go to the bar. Or you just might be tempted to have a go at the STW? Quiz which we usually featured in our programmes, a challenge to seat-bound, dieting teetotallers.

18. A Review of the Revue (Continued)

Here's the Second Half – Another Twelve Numbers chosen at random.

The Baillie on the Bench

The character who came to be known as Councillor Swick[1], having made the transition from the old Revue Group shows, found himself in many situations in STW? over the years, but if I were to choose my favourite Swick number it would have to be the one in which we promoted him to Baillie so that he could sit as presiding magistrate in the Police and later the District Court. This was how he first appeared when played by George Reid in the Student Show *Running Riot* in 1968 and the script had changed very little by the time Buff came to play him in STW? a few years later.

---

[1] Other Councillor Swick appearances:
  The Prizegiving
  At the Hustings
  The Auchterturra By-Election
  The World Bowling Championships
  Hogmanay in Auchterturra
  Press Conference
  The New M.P.

He had been born way, way back in 1961 in the first piece Buff and I had ever written together for the Revue Group show *Come What May*. Neatly described in an early newspaper article as "the unlettered local politician", his inaugural duty was to give the speech and hand out the awards at an end-of-term school prize-giving. Although firmly rooted in Aberdeen it emerged, judging from audience response away from home, that Councillor Swick strode the land, even into deepest Englandshire we were told, where he might be known as an alderman and have a different accent. Anyway Buff and I based him on an amalgam of people, although there is no doubt that the original idea was the annual appearance of Aberdeen's legendary Lord Provost Tommy Mitchell at the prize-giving ceremonies of both Robert Gordon's College and the Aberdeen Grammar School in the late Forties.

"Now," he would declaim, "to the many boys not on the prize list today, I would say this – I never won a prize in my life at the school, but I hinna deen nae badly."

Elevated then to the bench – behind which, as I recall, he tripped, disappeared and then reappeared Chad-like when played by George Reid (but not when played by Buff, whose physical comedy was limited to two or three facial expressions – well, two) – Baillie Swick cut a figure of commanding and glorious pomposity.

Although I say it myself, Swick had some great lines and Buff was on top form, but the number is notable also for a profusion of personal references, local and national depending on venue. So well known as a court lawyer was my good friend Frank Lefevre, (also businessman, entrepreneur, restaurateur, song writer, sportsman, charities supporter, etc., etc.) that he was perhaps the only permanent fixture in the sketch and, though his highly successful career required no help from STW?, it was interesting that an oilman returning to America put some Aberdeen business Mr Lefevre's way on the strength of the reference to him on one of our tapes. And when one day Frank, chancing to bump into Graham our business manager, threatened to sue us for defamation, Graham's response was that a counter claim might well follow for the publicity we had given him.

Spanish Holiday

Of all Buff's parodies, this one to the tune of *Granada* must be the cheapest and cheeriest – and that's a big compliment. Lacking any semblance of sophistication it was doon, doon, doon doonmarket and, performed as a threesome with daft sombreros, its appeal was simple, direct and hit straight to the funny bone of anyone who has any knowledge of the package trip to Costa del Tacky. Even done as a twosome in cabaret after Buff had called it a day, George and I found that the element of surprise attack it provided to the repertoire worked well and was rewarded by an abundance of easy-peasy laughs.

The Will

This is one of a number of our two-hander sketches in which the familiar music-hall terminology 'comic and feed' might be altered to 'Doric and feed'[2]. That's to say we would set up a situation in which Buff played a very neutral character feeding questions to a rustic worthy who had all the funny lines. It is a stock formula, not just tried and tested, but rather tired and tested, and I used to feel ambivalent about it. It is always nice to get laughs, but I found the method of doing so just a little too artificial. It was embarrassing, too, that I didn't have to work very hard.

The real slog was Buff's in the self-effacing role of feed; he it was who had the job of controlling the situation and getting the pace right, of remembering all these long questions carefully contrived to produce as simple and uncluttered and as funny a reply as possible.

The other aspect of the classic relationship between comic and feed is that the feed starts off by being the dominant character, the comic the inferior one, put upon and patronised. Gradually however, things turn out to be not quite as they seem and the roles of loser and winner are reversed. Nowhere is this seen more clearly than in *The Will* where the *sang-froid* of the solicitor is gradually eroded and finally destroyed by the outwardly ingenuous, innately shrewd old farmer.

---

[2] Other examples of 'Doric and feed' are:
Parents' Night
The Professor and the Builder
Mastermind
Desert Island Discs
The Fund-raiser
The Doric Parrot.

Having denigrated the Doric and feed situation in general terms I should temper my criticism of *The Will*. There is rather more to it than most Doric and feed sketches, if only because the situation is real. I know, because I have been in it many times, and although the venerable Mr Christie is not based on any particular person, there are chips off him in many an old country bloke who used to sit across the desk from me issuing his testamentary instructions. In another way too – a strangely physical way – I feel I know Mr Christie.

We did this sketch on our television show at Hogmanay 1985 and as the make-up girl completed her magic tricks I thought the octogenarian staring back at me in the mirror looked vaguely familiar. A day or two after the programme was shown I was visiting my elderly parents and my old man confirmed whose likeness it was I had seen. "It's a funny business," he said, "watching TV and seeing the spitting image of my father and your grandfather when the old devil's been dead for nearly forty years."

Ice Cream

This number is both rare and frequent. It is one of the few which began not with the words but the tune and it is one of quite a few which George is called upon to perform very often indeed. And does so happily to consummately humorous effect. He told the story of its conception when I was involved with the Aboyne & Deeside Festival a few years ago and managed to persuade him and Buff to do an evening together which was devoted to the music and lyrics of STW? It was a good idea on my part, because they attracted a full house and provided an entertainment which was also an education.

Even I, their closest colleague, familiar with their work for so long, gained insights and learned wee secrets as I watched and listened admiringly from the back of the auditorium.

Actually George's melody, he disclosed, was based on a pastiche which had been rolling around in his head for long enough, inspired by his friendship with the proprietor of an Italian ice-cream shop in his home town of Huntly who always greeted him with great warmth in a language all his own – not broken English, but critically fractured Doric.

"Foo're ye aye deein' Georgie, ma bambino loonie? Ye'll be for an ice-da-cream for a coola belly on this a warm-a-day?"

My favourite laugh-lines:

But Italian ice-a-cream cafés
Are a-gravely threatened nowadays.
For there is other nationalities
Invadin' oor patch – a...
Me I canna live
If it gets much mair competitive
These foreigners all should be deported.
I'd kick oot that lot
Fan ye think o't, fit a nerve they've got
Neen o' these can ever be
A native Scot-a like-a me. (Fortissimo)

Coal

As I was saying way back in Chapter 12, Buff and I played two stilted characters seated before a coal fire with not a thought between them that was not just feeble and ailing, but virtually dead and buried. And yet there was respect between Mr Taylor and Mr Wallace as demonstrated by their courteous use of each other's surnames. Although they went on to appear in half-a-dozen sketches[3] they never reached the friendship of Christian names. They might have been neighbours or work colleagues or just happened to meet in the street, but there was always a polite distance between them.

They actually began life as part of a foursome in the Aberdeen Revue Group's final show in 1967 *Going, Going...* (although some of us never quite went). The other parts, those of Mrs Taylor and Mrs Wallace, were played by Mrs Hardie and Mrs Logan – extremely well, I remember – and the sketch was such a success that we revived it as a two-hander for STW? several years later. Thus restricted, the relationship between Mr Wallace (the misinformed idiot) and Mr Taylor (the informed idiot) developed

[3] Other sketches featuring Mr Taylor and Mr Wallace:
The Supermarket
Under the Carpet
At the Airport
The Stop-Go Man
At the Palace
The Grandfather.

quite by accident in such a way that Mr Taylor made jokey remarks which Mr Wallace didn't understand. This was quite a bonus because there was a good chance that in a theatre full of folk, at least some would laugh at Mr Taylor's initial quip (no matter how painful it might be, the I.Q. of your average audience ranging as it does from a rare A to a numerous Z). If they didn't laugh, then for certain a larger number would laugh at Mr Wallace's lack of comprehension and stupid response. Another plus was the dip – again quite fortuitous – into metaphysics and the time warp. At which point, I have to say, I cannot believe I am writing this stuff, but humour does lie in the strangest places.

Bothy Ballad for a Roustabout

Although we knew very little about the oil industry beyond the headlines in the papers and on the box, we felt we had to respond to the odd accusation that this was of such huge national import, and on our own doorstep, that it was crying out for a humorous slant that had local associations.

So, what could be more local to the North-East of Scotland than the bothy ballad or cornkister? And, having heard of the migration to the oil rigs of so many workers from all sorts of other jobs attracted by the high wages, we thought it appropriate that one of these would be from the farming community, the orra loon traditionally featured in farm-town story and song.

I take no credit for being sufficiently energised by these links to start writing a few lines myself, since I very soon handed over to the expert himself, Mr Hardie, to do the job properly, but at least I chanced on the tune which lent itself to the treatment. This wasn't, strictly speaking, bothy ballad music, but came from the archives of Dr David Rorie[4]. It was the

---

[4] Dr David Rorie (1867-1946). As well as being a medical man of distinction, David Rorie was also a soldier who emerged from the First World War as Acting Colonel and Chevalier de Legion d'Honneur with a DSO and two mentions in dispatches. His memory lives on chiefly, however, through a third career – that of writer. He was a poet, lyricist, folklorist, humorist and composer, his best work being perhaps, not *The Pawky Duke*, but *The Lum Hat Wantin' A Croon*, which remains the signature tune of The Aberdeen Medical Chirurgical Society and is robustly aired at the Society's Annual Dinner.

tune to the tale of *The Pawky Duke* and was fit for the purpose of carrying the tale of our own hero, Lubin Jock McRafferty frae Mains o' Tillyscatterty.

Actually our version of Dr Rorie's song was in part rather saucy, referring as it did, to Peterhead's emergence as the glittering sin city of Buchan where resided a "Fille de joie – an' I chauve awa', an' I think that I dae ma work well. It's maybe nae fair, but I'm makin' much mair, than I did at Cross & Blackwell."

Sample favourite line:

Says the sonsy lass – ye've tae pay in cash
In sterling, gold or dollars – an'
For anither ten p, plus VAT
I jist micht tak' oot ma rollers.

Arrival and Departure

The success of Mr Taylor and Mr Wallace as Aiberdeen mannies – 'toon's dirt,' if you like – suggested that there might be a future for their country equivalents. Although Buff had reservations about his ability to do a Doric accent I was not discouraged, knowing that his reservations were par for the course. I managed to persuade him at last to have a go on the basis that we wouldn't give his character much to say, relying more on that innate talent of his, a face built as a force of nature to be totally dead-pan.

Thus, the lugubrious Norman and the perky Alec – Auchterturra's finest – were created and made their debut in a sketch called, appropriately enough, *Arrival*. It took place on Alec's doorstep and it seemed logical that, after a suitable interval – say two or three numbers, not a long enough time for the audience to forget who the characters were – Norman and Alec[5] should again appear on the doorstep to take a prolonged and agonising farewell.

Fortunately Norman and Alec seemed to go down pretty well with audiences, so they became permanent fixtures in the show and even had

---

[5] Other Norman and Alec sketches:
In the Garden
The Operation
Retirement

the central roles in the TV special we did for Grampian for Hogmanay 1992 when it was broadcast across the Midnight Bells. But that's a story for another place…

The Scottish Plumber

Andy Stewart was a huge name in Scottish show business in the early Sixties, a young man who shot to fame on television through The White Heather Club. This was popular entertainment, no doubt about it; unpretentious and homely, but at a cost.

It did much to perpetuate the myth throughout the U.K. that Scotland was a land artistically stilted by the heederum-hoderums, smarty kilts and a mish-mash of corny dancing and spurious tradition.

And at the heart of it, forever identified as representing Scotland, was poor Andy. It is possible to say "poor" Andy now, but not then, so big was he.

He had great talent, but for reasons of fortune and fame of a dubious kind, he followed the easy road of playing to the cheap seats, of dumbing down to that lowest common denominator which made him an object of scorn for a lot of people of reasonable intelligence, irrespective of whether they were in or out of Scotland.

Among such armchair critics were the new writers of the Aberdeen Revue Group, Hardie & Robertson, who could hardly wait to take their own less than respectful look at B.B.C. Scotland's transmission of what I remember describing with all the brassness of youth plus a tinge of envy as "a load of rubbish". And this was epitomised by Andy's rendition of the song, *The Scottish Soldier*, based on an old pipe tune, but romanticised by words written by Andy himself. It began, "There was a soldier, a Scottish soldier, who wandered far away…"

I well remember Buff, much drink taken on a Hogmanay, driving home with Eva and myself from somewhere in the country, spontaneously, impromptu and amid much laughter making the not so subtle, mickey-taking change as follows: "There was a plumber, a Scottish plumber, No finer man than he, To mend your wc…" and so on.

After we had dropped him off at home Buff, still in the mood, finished the parody off and presented it mint fresh at our next meeting, suggesting I might try an impersonation. Which I was delighted to do. Andy was not difficult, I found, and so *The Scottish Plumber* won its place in the works of the old Aberdeen Revue Group and then in STW?

At first he featured in the Revue Group version of The White Heather Club, other satirical Hardie parodies applying to such weel kent performers as Dixie Ingram, a nifty hoofer, Jimmy Shand the accordionist, Alastair McHarg, a wobbly baritone who went to Australia, and James Urquhart, a wobbly tenor who remained in Fife.

On the distaff side there was a troupe of lassies who danced perjinkly, some bonnier than others, and occasional guest singers such as Moira Anderson and our own good friends Anne and Laura Brand who we, totally unbiased, thought added much-needed quality to the proceedings.[6]

Later in STW? Andy found himself over the years – because we were always able to find some reason for bringing him back along with other tartan pals – accompanied by familiar names like Calum Kennedy, the afore-mentioned Moira Anderson, Kenneth McKellar, Jim McLeod and most memorably, The Alexander Brothers. Andy even tried a fresh parody written for him by Buff in one of our summer seasons. *Donald Whaur's yer Troosers* became *Nona, Far's yer Knickers*, based on a newspaper scandal involving Edinburgh M.P. Ron Brown. This prompted one of the few objections we ever experienced about STW? containing offensive material.

Maybe critics didn't look hard enough.

Jimmy Carter, 1978

Still on the subject of impudent take-offs, I never have found out the difference between an impression and an impersonation. 'Impersonation' has overtones of criminality and sounds less artistic; 'impression' sounds all too artistic, however, for the kind of verbal caricature in which I dabbled, and not always successfully. I think I got away with Jimmy Carter because he was intrinsically a pleasant guy. Even if I was not very accurate, the script was strong, and his character was broad enough and amiable enough for the audience to like.

That was not the case with the late Enoch Powell and Tony Benn. On

---

[6] And at the same time as *The White Heather Club* was happening on BBC Scotland we, clever dicks that we were, scarcely beyond appreciation of undergraduate humour, had become avid fans of *That Was The Week That Was* (though I must admit I always found David Frost's drawling presentation highly resistible). The shows were chalk and cheese, from different planets rather than different countries.

our second trip to the Edinburgh Festival I learned a long Enoch Powell piece which was an unmitigated disaster. It is a painful business trying to sustain simultaneously a wild stare and an educated Midland accent, all the while wearing a gloomy homburg hat slightly too large for one's nut, without the comforting punctuation of audience laughter. Enoch was just too serious to be funny and lasted only three nights. I have been deeply prejudiced against him ever since.

The fact that Tony Benn lasted only one night gives you an indication of how strongly I feel about him. The trouble was the same. No matter how good or bad the mimicry, Tony was too intense for the audience to warm to. He either didn't have, or I failed to find in him, a comic dimension. Mind you, Rory Bremner managed it in more recent years. But then he really is a comic genius!

Someone who did have a laughable dimension whom I 'did' in the same show, was Colonel Mad Mitch, a very controversial figure; a high-profile ex-Argyll who was MP for West Aberdeenshire. I am sure I did not 'get' him all that closely – the clipped military voice oozing authority was probably enough – but the number was a great success because the character was bright and crisp and, just as important, Buff's idea of turning the House of Commons into a parade for him to command was not bad either.

"House of Commons! Attention!" he snapped. "As you were: Now I don't know what you think you're on, but you're a scruffy, idle, dozy lot and I want you to do that again. House of Commons! Attention! That's better. Stand still. Who's that man grinning? What's your name? Heath, eh? Take that smile off your face, Heath…" and so on.

These words have come tumbling off the top of my head which is normally a sign of something worthwhile. I could not for the life of me remember a syllable of Enoch or Tony.

Over the years I have tried to 'do' people with varying success. I saw this as a peripheral contribution to STW?, part of our attempt to keep the texture as interesting as the straitjacket of a three-man show would allow. But the only person I remember getting a real buzz from mimicking was Sir Alec Douglas Home, as he was known when he first came to prominence on our black-and-white television screens as the new Prime Minister. He seemed to me a most amusing old stick and for no reason other than the immediate fun of it I instinctively copied the voice. Standing in front of the bathroom mirror I pulled faces until it dawned on me that the way to assume his most marked characteristic, literally the stiff upper lip, might be to stuff wads of toilet paper above my upper front teeth. As I jammed the paper in I knew I had done the trick. I felt transmogrified and transported. This was a real creative kick and I could scarcely stop myself falling about at the image waffling back at me between the toothbrushes and the tumbler.

Sir Alec and the script we wrote for him addressing the haggis at the Old Etonian Burns Supper have stood us in good stead ever since. Even after Sir Alec faded from the public eye we could not bring ourselves to abandon the idea of the Haggis being addressed in a frightfully posh English accent and found a ready substitution in the person of the Chief Executive of the Scottish Tourist Board. Alan Devereux, gentleman that he was, didn't seem to mind a bit because we were honoured by an invitation to do the cabaret in the Grosvenor Hotel, Glasgow for his retiral dinner.

How Are Things in Auchterturra?

Even now, nearly fifty years after becoming W.D. Hardie's writing partner (and as I pen these words we still get together once a month to do the script for the Councillor Swick cartoon in *Leopard* magazine), I can still get an uneasy feeling when an idea, a line, a word or thought I have come up with is confronted by a blank look from eyes of deepest black. The expression can be more than dead-pan. It can look hostile and scary and although I know in my head that the great man is the softest pussy-cat in nature, that he is only giving what I have dared to suggest the benefit of full and careful consideration, it is a relief nevertheless, after what can be an interminable pause, to get any kind of response from him which is not totally negative.

So it was more than twenty years ago, when I expressed the notion that the hit song *How Are Things in Glocca Morra* from *Finian's Rainbow* might lend itself to parody, that I waited with bated breath for the magisterial reply and was not surprised when it was by no means positive. My recollection is that he was not even all that happy with the idea, which I have to say I was very confident about; and just as confident that Buff could make a terrific job of it.

And, of course, he did. He came back a couple of days later to expose the extraordinary result to James and myself – a number for the three of us to share, George free to catch the mood of the piece with his piano arrangement while Buff and I conducted a phone conversation between far-away exile and local…

> EXILE:
> *"I'm in Hong Kong*
> *But nostalgia's strong*
> *I'd like a crack*
> *With someone back*
> *Where I belong."*
> LOCAL:
> *"That's the phone for me*
> *Wonder fa' it can be*
> *Hullo, who's there?*
> *This is Auchterturra two-one-three."*

And so on, a bitter-sweet, funny lament for a way of life that was better in precisely specified ways than those now foisted on a small rural community by the powers that be. It is a gem of a song, to which I think the three of us did justice in performance, and since it carried so lightly and almost incidentally something of a social message, it became a big favourite among audiences everywhere.

And an even bigger favourite among ourselves as performers. For myself particularly and rather selfishly it was a joy to do, since as the local lad in Auchterturra I was getting all the laughs. But more than that, I was aware of the privilege of sharing the stage with a brilliant pianist and a superlative lyricist who both just happened to be my close friends.

You cannot ask for better than that.

The Auchterturra Election

As writers, Buff and I used to have a list of ideas at the back of the notebook – subjects to examine at some future date which might win a chuckle or two if suitably treated. One which had been hiding away there for years was the ritual of the Declaration at a parliamentary election, which always struck us as ripe for a take-off. That was the starting point for this number which proceeded, as a series of snippets, to grow and grow; and all quite logically.

There could not be a Declaration without Councillor Swick to go

"Come in, Norman."
"No, I'm nae comin' in."

PHOTO: ABERDEEN JOURNALS

through the rigmarole of announcing the winner and nobody would be more suitable for giving an Acceptance speech than Sandy Thomson, whom we had often wanted to see sharing a sketch with the good councillor anyway. By this time Buff had written the lyric, *How Are Things in Auchterturra*, so Auchterturra therefore became the location for the momentous political event.

Independent of all this I rather fancied doing an impression or two just because I had not done any for a while, so this seemed as good an opportunity as any. The odd item, as short as possible, could be tucked in without too much damage being done, hence the reason for John Cole, sometime political editor for the BBC, introducing the sketch as "A parliamentary by-election Special for *Newsnight*", and Ian MacAskill, popular weatherman of the day, giving his Auchterturra forecast.

Then not to be outshone by such dubious virtuosity, Buff insisted on doing his bravura impersonation of Sir Alastair Burnett, famous newscaster, to link the material. And finally, in order to give a musical full-stop to the whole interminable epic, we remembered that we had one song with vaguely political associations, *Dalyell's Awa' Wi the Fairies*, a parody of *The De'il's Awa wi' the Exciseman*. This was hastily adapted so that George could be brought on before the audience forgot about him altogether – roused from his chaise-longue in the dressing-room where he might otherwise have slept on, sated by chocolates and Glenmorangie.

Scottish Nightmare and Reputations

Here's another example of George writing the tune before Buff wrote the words, but in a different way. Going back to the Revue Group show 1964, George had composed the music for Buff's lyric entitled *Royal Babies* which began:

> *Four new royal babies[7]*
> *In ninety sixty-four*
> *And we who pay the taxes*
> *Pray there will be no more…*

…and it was this tune which was so cheekily right in 1971 for an idea of James's, namely to explore the stereotyped myths about Scotland portrayed in song. After starting to explore that territory Buff found himself venturing into wider fields, casting doubt on whether he was focusing on Scottish Nightmares or just Myths. Not that it really mattered, the only true test being whether there was a laugh from the audience or not.

One thing led to another and a further development of the theme – using the same impudent, bouncy tune – was the thought that a lot of people, whether Scottish or Timbucktooean, were assuredly not what they appeared to be. This chimed perfectly with the concept of STW? and thus provided a most satisfactory ending or near-ending to a light-hearted evening. Topicality was essential and the phrases could be changed by Buff, as readily as he changed his socks, to accommodate an up-to-date reference to someone in the news. Here's how one or two of the more

[7] The four certainly included Prince Edward, but the other three? Sorry, cannot remember and they will almost certainly be off the Civil List by this time anyway.

We always ended the show in black ties – even matinées *en pleine air*

successful lines went after the arresting set-up verse:

> *Public reputations are often wrong you'll find,*
> *We've got some revelations to really blow your mind.*
> *Regan's really youthful,*
> *Chernenko's in the pink,*
> *The Ayatollah Khomenei*
> *Taks a helluva drink.*
> *Looking back through history*
> *The legends melt awa'*
> *The fiery revolution'ries*
> *Were nae like that at a';*
>
> *Lenin was a capitalist*
> *Gandhi wore a suit*
> *Chairman Mao was the owner*
> *Of a Chinese carry-oot.*

Pope John Paul the Second
Is a Rangers fan.
Sylvester Stallone is gay
And Dolly Parton is a man.

But the strangest reputation
Is the one that Scotland's got
When folk sing Scotland the Brave,
We say "Scotland the What?"

Part Four

STW?
The Cottage
Industry

Preface

STW? was, first and last, a live stage show. That's how it began and that's how it ended, but growing out of our live appearances, there fell into our lucky laps other opportunities – collateral benefits, or added value – since we were, after all, in the business of trying to make a decent living.

Of these offshoots the main one was television from which sprang videos and ultimately a DVD, but there were also a couple of books and lots of records which became cassettes which became CDs. Then, less well known in their day and completely forgotten now, we did a bit of radio, quite a few advertisements and, for no reward except a dram or two and the wee thrill of seeing the name of STW? associated with it, we co-operated with Teacher's – the grand old whisky company – in having a malt produced called *The Auchterturra*.

The label read:

Distilled in 1969
THE AUCHTERTURRA
Pure Highland Malt Whisky
This product was distilled just beyond the back of beyond
at Auchterturra, by Rhynie, Huntly, Aberdeenshire.
It was specially bottled for the bow-tied stalwarts of STW? and gives them
courage before, and comfort after, facing a hostile audience.[1]

So you see, the audience, hostile or friendly, suspicious, indifferent or sometimes even enthusiastic – the live audience was very much part of the live experience of STW? which was the core business of what became our cottage industry. The rest of that cottage industry does, however, deserve some attention.

[1] 'The Auchterturra' was not for sale. As well as being for our own enjoyment (stocks now virtually exhausted – I believe George and Buff just might have half a bottle hidden away, but mine are long gone) it was a very handy gift not only on private occasions, but on public ones when it was frequently offered for raffle or auction. Looking back you might call it a public relations tool, but we never thought of it that way.

19. STW? and Television:
The Best and the Worst...

**"When you do the show on stage, taking it to
as many theatres as you like, you're playing
to a few thousand people. If you do it on television
you're playing to more than a million"**
—Alan Franchi, Grampian Television Director

By far the best thing that happened to myself through television – and I am pretty sure this goes for Buff and George too – was the friendship that developed with Alan and his wife Jane. When James Logan decided to retire early in 1993 he was very much involved in the appointment and take-over of his successor, Alan, with whom we had all got on so well as Director of our Grampian shows and who was himself due to retire from Grampian within the next year or so. It was a very natural progression with which Alan seemed as pleased as we were. So it was that he and Jane became part of the STW? family and cottage industry.

Actually it was not Alan in the first instance who persuaded us to 'do television again,[1] leading to all those Hogmanay shows of which he was the Director.[2] The man who cheerfully argued us out of our suspicions towards the medium was John Hughes, the bright and breezy Controller

On our travels with Alan, the best of friends.   PHOTO: GORDON WRIGHT

of Grampian in the mid-Eighties.

Many's the social encounter we had with John, usually over his favoured pot of tea, and while he didn't interfere with our programmes once they were into production and under Alan's control, he certainly made a contribution beforehand and kept a weather eye on the situation in the way of a real pro steeped in the business, going right back to the

---

[1] 'Again?' Individually or collectively we had 'done' quite a bit of television for both the BBC and Grampian long before Grampian's latest invitation and were pretty cool about it, mainly because it used up so much material.

[2] As well as our own annual show and an Edinburgh Festival Special we participated in several other mixed bill Hogmanay programmes between 1985 and 1996, usually outside broadcasts from such splendid locations as Glamis and Blair Atholl Castles and Scone Palace.

black and white days of *Dixon of Dock Green*. He was a thoroughly good sort and we were very sorry indeed to learn before our own retirement that he had parted company with Grampian on rather sad terms. And then not so long after that we were further saddened to learn that he had died. George could not make it from Perth, but it was a privilege for Alan, Buff and myself to pay our respects at his funeral, where it was disappointing to note that Grampian's hierarchy was not well represented.

But back to working with Alan… And here a lot of sadness comes into the picture because just as I was about to start the rather tedious business of proof-reading this narrative we received the shocking news of his sudden illness and death. The date was 24th August 2010, and at the funeral service in an overflowing crematorium a week later George, Buff and I, on behalf of the STW? family, were honoured to be asked by Jane to join Alan's nephew Neil on behalf of his side of the family, her sister Susie on her side, and Jimmy Spankie on behalf of the Grampian Television family, in paying tribute to a consummate gentleman and a most loveable human being. I hope we all did him justice, but if not the 'After Show Party' given by Jane in Dizzy's, Alan's favourite watering-hole, certainly made up for it, buzzing as it was with "Laughter and the love and kindness of friends".

If the connection with Alan was the best thing that happened through television – and local Grampian takes the credit – the worst thing that happened was to do with their national rivals. In the early summer of 1984 we had taken part in a BBC series called *Halls of Fame*, one of the Halls being our own HMT where we had enjoyed meeting, among others on the bill, such names as Andrew Cruickshank, Andy Stewart, Billy Dainty, Chic Murray, Roy Hudd and Bill Pertwee.

That had all gone fine and it must have been on the strength of that that we were invited to be on the BBC Hogmanay Show, to be broadcast from Gleneagles. Well, that sounded just great, particularly since we were to be appearing a few days later at the Queen Elizabeth Hall on London's South Bank and thought that the national exposure would do us no harm at all.

Mind you, George who was not included in the invitation – comedy without music being the producer's requirement – did strike a note of caution, based on a suspicion of mixed bills where we weren't on long enough for our style and material to generate their own atmosphere.

"I'm not sure it is your scene lads," was his gentle warning – and he was right, but only partly so. It turned out not to be anybody's scene – except that of the Press critics who gloried in their own powers of vituperation about what turned out to be "a turkey to the wattles", to quote a phrase from one of them, a phrase sufficiently original and colourful for me to remember it all these years later. It must certainly remain in BBC lore as one of their greatest unmitigated disasters of all time and for our own part, Buff and I found it an unhappy experience.

With the benefit of hindsight we should have been more sensitive to George's suspicions and other warning signs. "Pride cometh...etc.," but actually pride at being asked was no more a factor in our acceptance than the assumption that we would be put up at Gleneagles, and maybe the wives would be able to accompany us, and there would be a window, perhaps, for a pleasant meal – which wouldn't be a bad way of spending Hogmanay in exchange for one five-minute spot of our own choice on the show. That spot we would ensure was something we knew backwards which would cause a minimum of worry or butterflies; and even if the fee was not marvellous the network appearance would make up for it.

The first premonition of doom was the withdrawal of one of the acts. Bucks Fizz was a middle-of-the-road group enjoying great popularity at the time and their involvement in a bad road accident a few days before had left them all terribly shaken and one of them hospitalised for many months. We then learned that, far from being given the star treatment at Gleneagles, we were being offered accommodation at the pub in Blackford several miles away. No disrespect to the pub, but it was hardly Gleneagles. Nor, speaking personally, was the prospect of sharing a room too attractive, having regard to the decibel level of W.D. Hardie's stertorous slumbers.

These were matters of minor significance, however. We would have to forget about any pleasurable sideshows and concentrate on the job in hand, following which we would high-tail it to Perth and get a bed at George's.

Humbly presenting ourselves at Gleneagles on the afternoon of 31st December 1984, we found the place like a fortress besieged. The serious dark green of the BBC trucks seemed to surround the building and the army of technocrats had already invaded. Even in the best run television show it is useful for the performer to have a capacity for suffering. There is a lot of boredom, a lot of hanging about, a lot of stress and tension before the sudden release of adrenaline and nervous energy. What there is not a lot of is consideration for the performer on the part of the busy director and his technical battalions who all have their own job to do, large or small. And the bigger the outfit the smaller some of the jobs are.

So there, at Gleneagles that Hogmanay, there seemed to be too many people doing too many small jobs – overstaffing was certainly a BBC problem in those days – and all under the charge of a Director whose grip on the situation was exemplified in our case by the fact that he barely gave us the time of day, far less offered any words of advice or encouragement. The trouble probably began at a higher level. It was not clear whether the party being broadcast was a Gleneagles affair at which the BBC cameras just happened to be present, or a BBC affair which just happened to be held at Gleneagles. This failure of communication led to a good deal of confusion.

The audience comprised mostly Gleneagles' guests who had paid sweetly for their New Year break, including the bonus of the broadcast entertainment, and getting their money's worth including behaving as they wished, not as the floor manager (on his cans from the Director) requested. In fact they didn't pay much attention to the performers, never mind the poor floor manager, so eager did they appear to be either to get in front of the cameras themselves, or to find a waiter for more drinks. The normal conventions for an audience were happily ignored by this lot and the result was chaos.

Survivors must have their own embattled memory of the turmoil. Mine is that when the time came for Buff and me to do our turn, we literally had to fight our way through the crowd to get on to the floor in front of the camera. Not that anybody was interested, a fact which was confirmed later when I bumped into an old friend in the bar, Ron Comber from schooldays, who claimed that he and his family had enjoyed our contribution, but nobody else seemed to be paying much attention. Anyway, Buff and I were the lucky ones, because at least we managed to get through our stuff and live to fight another day.[3]

Others were not so lucky. A well-respected old actor, John Grieve, having against all the odds managed to deliver a new and difficult-to-learn monologue, then proceeded to dry completely in the middle of one he'd

---

[3] We did a Doric and feed sketch which was a take-off of *Desert Island Discs*. Before Gleneagles it had been a favourite. After Gleneagles we never liked it again.

been doing for years. He was last to be seen after the show being led away weeping, supported by two nurse-like production assistants down a long, long corridor heading almost certainly for the nearest psychiatric ward.

Then the great Chic Murray got in a dreadful fankle looking for the microphone which was not where it should have been for one of his inimitable stand-up spots. Some viewers, less charitable than knowledgeable, suggested that he was the worse for drink, but it is impossible to be so affected by the soft drinks and tea to which (he sadly told us in the canteen) his doctor had restricted him because of a recurring virus. Chic never did find the mike; his second spot was cut and he pegged out a couple of months later, his death undoubtedly hastened by the trauma and ignominy which had befallen him because of the shortcomings of a loutish audience and back-up staff less professional than he.

It is always the people doing the comedy who have the smallest margin for error in terms of audience response. The host of the show, Tom O'Connor, would be the first to admit that he, like ourselves, died on his feet, but that was not so much his fault as that of whatever strange decision-making process in the BBC was responsible for him getting the job in the first place   a perky Liverpudlian link man on a prestigious, very Scottish occasion. As it was, fighting against all the odds, he did nobly to survive.

Without the need for audience laughter, singers and musicians have an easier time of it and so it was at Gleneagles. However, I think we learned the true meaning of Moira Anderson's OBE…Outraged Beyond Endurance – by the knowledge that despite the precaution she had taken of having the words of her songs chalked in capitals on a large blackboard just off camera, she was in a real stinker. The rest of the singing and music were provided by Bill Torrance the milk advert man, a bonny blonde lassie called Maggie Moon,[4] a pop group substituting for Bucks Fizz, now mercifully forgotten, and a pipe band which it is impossible to forget.

They contained drums too, like any pipe band worth their salt, and they looked and sounded amazing. There seemed a helluva lot of them and boy, did they give it laldy! As they marched into the ballroom a path was supposed to clear through the glittering audience. It didn't. The audience danced, the band marched. The irresistible force met the

---

[4] It later emerged that she gallantly coped simultaneously not only with her song, but also the groping attentions of some sozzled ass in the audience.

immovable object and the wailing sounds which resulted suggested there may have been terrible casualties. The television pictures were of a human maelstrom, uncontrollable, unstoppable, frozen in time as the credits rolled, but looking as if it would go on for ever.

Buff and I crept away into the night and drove to Perth in silence. George was waiting for us with large whiskies. "Sorry lads," he smiled sympathetically. "I did try to warn you."

20. STW? and Television:
After the Best and the Worst; the Rest

**"STW? are the most-highly paid performers
on Grampian, you know..."**
— Alan Franchi, confidentially after late-night refreshment

Well that was nice to know, I suppose, and all credit to the negotiating skills of our esteemed Business Manager who, come to think of it, has been the subject so far of the merest passing reference, and demands fuller attention. I can do no better then than reproduce the encomium written by Buff in that Charity Gala Programme of our closing season in 1995. Here it is and I agree with his every word except that, unsurprisingly, 14 years on Graham is now retired and Ledingham Chalmers are no longer at 1, Golden Square:

"Throughout the years our Business Manager has been Graham Hunter. Roped in to deal with the business side of the original expedition to the Edinburgh Festival Fringe in 1969, Graham confessed at that time to never having seen "the back-side of a show before". Still with us and still a close friend, all these years later, he sees no reason for revising that description of those parts of *Scotland the What?'s* activities which do not come before the eye of the public.

His contribution has been all that you would expect from a highly respected senior Aberdeen solicitor. Clerk and Assessor to the Seven Incorporated Trades of Aberdeen, inspiring University lecturer on that most inspiring of subjects, Full Repairing Leases, and a man regarded universally as the Perry Mason of the Licensing Court.

We have benefited enormously from his wide variety of skills: from his ability to produce a coherent and comprehensible minute of the discursive ramblings which pass for a *Scotland the What?* business meeting; from his

business-like assessment of our more fanciful notions; from his dexterity and finesse in personal relations which have made him the ideal interface between the show and theatre managements at all levels up and down the country; from his self-appointed roll as Mr Average Member of the Audience in which he gives perceptive and down-to-earth views on new material; from his congenial company and, occasionally from his suggestions for new ideas. He it was who, while looking out from the breakfast room in the Caledonian Hotel in Edinburgh, studied the castle for a moment and reflected, "I wonder if they ever got planning permission for that castle". The resultant sketch has served us well in Edinburgh and elsewhere over the years.

Graham in serious mode

To return to that first venture to the Edinburgh Festival Fringe in 1969, the show had been advertised as "including free oatcake". This idea, which seemed amusing when it occurred to us (late one evening over a dram), then had to be implemented when we got to Edinburgh, and it was unanimously agreed by the rest of us that this was a task appropriate to the business manager's function. To his undying credit, Graham did obtain a large supply of oatcakes at a knock-down wholesale price. Indeed he still has some left, so if you fancy one, please apply to him at Ledingham Chalmers, 1-17 Golden Square.

It may take you a while to get through to Graham but, when you do, you will be received with old-world charm, civility and fairness from the man who beyond the call of duty has been the indispensable rock on which the sometimes teetering edifice of *Scotland the What?* has leant.

Thanks, Graham."

More than that however, I would like to put on record an appreciation of Graham's talent for that kind of service beyond the call of duty which amounts to real friendship. There are probably more, but these examples come immediately to mind. The first was his presentation to the partners of STW? on our change of careers in 1983 when we went full-time, a carefully compiled scrap-book/memento of all that had happened to us from our beginnings at the Fringe in 1969 when we twisted his arm to join us.

The second was a similar presentation marking the years from 1983 to 2008 in which Graham was greatly helped by his wife Janet. These are not only gifts to treasure, but also reliable repositories of fact and detail which I have been able to consult in writing this, my own story of STW?

And the third memory to treasure took place in 1994 when we were the first recipients of a new honorary degree from Aberdeen University, that of M.Univ. – Masters of the University. That naturally called for a private celebration dinner at which Graham, who is known to cordially dislike having to make a formal speech, delivered himself of a toast to STW? – the show and the partners – which was both touching and beautifully expressed.

But back to the business of doing television programmes. When John Hughes charmed us back into Grampian's fold in 1985 we imposed on ourselves a discipline which was actually pretty easy. "Waste not, want not," had always been a jokey defence if we were accused of using old material in different situations and telly certainly gave us that excuse again. We would only do stuff that we had used already for the stage show.

Long before recycling became a fashionable badge of honour for ardent conservationists we were pioneers on Grampian. And that seemed to work pretty well since we kept being asked back every year – so often that it became almost a tradition that at least in the Grampian area STW? would be vying with the great Rikki Fulton and Scotch & Wry on the BBC in the ratings battle. Heady days indeed, and even headier when Rikki 'came round' to say hello when we were at the King's in Glasgow, and thus began a friendship which was, for us newcomers to the Central Belt and the mainstream of Scottish show business, an enormous privilege. He was a real gentleman and along with his delightful wife, Kate, hosted splendid parties at their home, way out the Great Western Road somewhere, where fellow guests would include such luminaries as Jimmy Logan and his wife, and Jack Milroy and Mary Lee.

There now, I am digressing again. These programmes we did for Grampian, invariably recorded a month or so before Hogmanay, were happy affairs for us in terms of preparation, rehearsal, actual performance before a live audience – and working relations. And particularly working relations. The entire crew or crews (because we're talking about a dozen shows over a ten-year period) could not, from top to bottom, have been more friendly and supportive. Comparisons are odious and obviously one had favourites (and they will maybe know who they are if they ever chance to read this) but they all, every single one of the people we worked with on these programmes, deserve a mention in the dispatches of a special footnote. Just a pity there is not room!

There were lots of laughs – and I don't mean the ones garnered in performance before the cameras. It is the things that go wrong in rehearsal; the malfunction of some piece of hardware – sound, lighting, whatever – caused by or affecting its operator; the in-jokes and back-chat of the scene-shifters; these were the stuff of the studio, generating humour and laughter. Buff, George and I enjoyed all of that, even the bits when we had to hang around while Alan from his lair in the control room or scanner endlessly tweaked quarter of a millimetre on a camera angle, or a marginally rosier flush from one of the lights.

And James too, who had been closely involved from the first planning of a programme, enjoyed being on hand, keeping a watching eye and offering a word on proceedings. He was very much in his element, too, just before a recording took place, when he was let loose on the audience to give them an idea of who, why and what was about to happen. He chatted knowledgeably and authoritatively without any authority, really, and not a lot of knowledge, but the point was that he put the audience at their ease – effortlessly. A born communicator, he was the ideal 'warm up' and often much more naturally funny than we three were in the programme that followed.

We must have been doing something right as far as Grampian's top brass were concerned because after several of our Hogmanay annuals – half-hour programmes shown during the run-up to midnight – we were offered the very prestigious slot 'across the bells'. This could have been a poisoned chalice, as indeed was the Gleneagles show for the BBC, but we decided to look upon it as a challenge and also an opportunity to break our 'waste not, want not' rule. We would have to write a new show, or at least devise one where some sketches and songs which had already had an airing on stage could be used, but only if they were relevant to the rest of the action.

So it was that *Hogmanay in Auchterturra* was conceived and brought into the world – well, not quite – into the Grampian area rather (and later adopted by STV) between 11pm on 31st December 1992 and 12.30am on 1st January 1993. From which you will hopefully infer that the action was supposed to be taking place live as the viewer at home watched, so that in the context of what passed for a plot, the bells did ring for midnight in real time – except that the location for the kirk steeple at Auchterturra was the kirk steeple at Rhynie, and the location for the kirk interior and pulpit at Auchterturra from which the minister was taking a late-night service, was the kirk interior and pulpit of Towie, Strathdon.

Actually we must have used a dozen or more locations as well as the studio, which rather reflected the ambition of the project. This was underlined also by the quality of performers we were able to sign up. They were, in no particular order, the late and much lamented George Duffus[1], Eileen McCallum, Ronnie Brown of the Corries, Robbie Shepherd, Charlie Allan, Colin Campbell, The McCalmans and Gordon McCulloch and his Band. We did also invite Evelyn Glennie to come and play the spoons, but unfortunately, although she said she would have loved to make it, she was kinda busy.

I must say we did get a lot of satisfaction out of producing that programme in which Buff and I played two of our favourite characters, Norman and Alec, who were out on the tiles first-footing. In the course of this they encounter various residents of the village, among whom were the names above-mentioned plus George Donald himself, who, playing the part of the Auchterturra dominie had his own musical contribution to add to the proceedings.

There is not much more to be said about Hogmanay in Auchterturra except that, after all the thought and effort that went into it, there was a feeling of anti-climax about it afterwards. When you are doing a show on

---

[1] George Duffus sadly died in February, 2002, too soon, far, far too soon. He was a lovely guy who became a really good and most generous friend when he and I found ourselves in the same HMT pantomime together over Christmas and the New Year 1990-91. Buff and George also got to know him and like him just as much on the after-dinner circuit where he was a very funny and accomplished speaker. Buff was one of those who paid most moving tributes to him at his funeral in St Andrew's Church, Dundee.

stage in front of a live audience there is the immediate gratification of laughter and applause and you get to take a bow at the end. The same applied even when we were recording our annual 'waste not, want not' shows in the TV studio.

But there was no live audience for Hogmanay in Auchterturra, no laughter or applause, no bow in acknowledgement or any kind of response, good or bad. The show just seemed to disappear without trace. I don't think it got even a passing reference in the local press. Maybe a few loyal souls mentioned that they'd enjoyed it, but very few – and that was it. Yet Alan Franchi said at lunch not so long ago that he had chanced on the tape the night before and played it out of nostalgic interest, and that it stood up very well, was really very good. I haven't seen it again myself, but if I were tempted I know I would wince with embarrassment, because that's my usual response any time I see myself on the box. It is to do with vanity, I suppose. Surely I am better looking than that guy on the telly screen who, come to think of it, isn't giving a very convincing performance either.

Hogmanay in Auchterturra was not the only programme we devised specially for Grampian. I had almost forgotten that a couple of years earlier Alan and his cheery crew followed us down to Edinburgh where we were appearing at the King's in a late-night Festival show. This was an opportunity not only to record excerpts played live in the theatre, but also to go out and about playing various character parts and, in character, meeting different people.

Of these the best-known was Ricky Demarco, in his inimitable way the very spirit, life and soul of the Edinburgh Festival, who had several things going on in an old building just off the Royal Mile. One I particularly remember was an Art exhibition.

A very modern Art exhibition. From somewhere in Eastern Europe, I think, and Buff and I, playing our favourite Aberdeen mannies Mr Taylor and Mr Wallace seeking culture, had chanced on this Mecca of the bizarre and on its resident promoter, Ricky. Not just its promoter, but an Art expert for whom we wrote a few lines of amusing dialogue. However, it was not half – no, a tenth – as funny as rehearsal with Ricky.

If I was to select the top five funniest situations I have ever experienced, that encounter with Ricky would have to be among them. Near the top. Maybe equal top. He was hilarious. Buff and I fell about, rolled on the floor, honestly, at his attempts to deliver the lines we had written. Try as he might to be natural and conversational in front of a camera, he tied himself in tortured knots. The harder and the more seriously he tried, the worse – and funnier – he became. Actor Ricky was not. It is ironic that someone who is in complete control of his own complex subject could be so lacking in the simple job of reading a few words off a script. Not that we were all that marvellous – and our knowledge of modern Art was certainly less than his of how to deliver a line.

The episode ended happily when we met up with Ricky for supper later at an Italian restaurant of his discriminating choice after our evening show at the King's. He was delightful company, along with a few other sociable souls we had gathered up in our television travels.

Most outrageous of these was an illusionist called Fay Presto who did tricks at the table and who cut a colourful figure rather symbolic of the Festival as a whole. She was free and easy; worldly wise and casually elegant from top to toe – all six feet of her. At least. And she was adaptable. Having discovered that she was not drawing many customers in the venue she had booked, she had gone busking, doing her show in the open air from a smart platform created from the boot of her car, a rather splendid affair. It was a Vanden Plas Austin Princess of Fifties vintage, known in its day as 'the poor man's Rolls Royce'.

This is an appropriate cue to reveal our suspicion that this formidable but glamorous dame might well be a fella. Whatever the gender, this strolling player fairly brought a touch of the exotic to our bourgeois lives that extraordinary week – extraordinary also as it was so busy for us. We weren't used to the pressure.

Since going full-time we had had plenty experience of writing and preparing and working a show, then performing it on stage, a fairly leisurely process. Likewise we did not exactly bust a gut when involved in the exercise of doing a television show. But this particular week we were out and about filming in many diverse locations during the day and then in the evening doing our stage show at the King's.

I can only reiterate the weary words with which I replied to Eva when I got home on the Sunday and she asked how everything had gone. "Well dear," I said. "I haven't had such a hard week since I was working as a bloody solicitor."

21. STW? and Television:
After the Best, the Worst and the Rest, a Couple that Didn't Go Out at All

**"We'd like you to meet Tom Fleming.
He's presenting a programme to celebrate
the Queen Mother's Eightieth Birthday."**
— BBC producer on the phone, June 1980

Well, that was some invitation, certainly not one to be sniffed at, so off we went to Glasgow to have lunch with a most distinguished gentleman of the theatre and broadcasting.

Although Tom Fleming had made his name as an actor – he had distant memories of his beginnings as a spear-carrier at Stratford with the RSC – it was as a broadcaster that he found more popular success.

He had made his own the presentation of any programme of national pomp, circumstance and ceremony, particularly when a royal personage was involved. It was the received wisdom that he was the Queen Mother's favourite broadcaster and that was why he was at the heart of her prestigious birthday programme.

But why did STW? and I in particular get the call? Well, it was all that chap Sandy Thomson's fault. His was the plain vanilla name we had chosen to make all these phone-calls to members of the Royal family.

Word had reached the ears of the Beeb and Sir Tom[1] (well, that's how I thought of him after, in courtly fashion, he had hosted a most civilised albeit modest lunch in the majestic surroundings of the BBC Canteen). And it was not surprising that they had heard of our efforts, since the phone-call to Her Majesty inviting her "to come and open the Oldmeldrum Sports a wik on Setterday" had appeared on Grampian's Hogmanay programme a couple of years previously. This was not our own 'waste not, want not' contribution which would have been put out sometime mid-evening, but the one in the midnight slot which was being networked live and in which I was flattered to be invited to appear.

And now it was even more flattering to be in the frame for a possible appearance on the Queen Mum programme with a suitably adapted script for another phone-call. But it didn't happen. After our pleasant lunch I did a recording of what we had prepared (and got paid for my trouble) but was sorry when the broadcast was made to note that I had been "left on the cutting room floor", as they say in the best film circles. Never mind, it was an interesting experience and an especial pleasure to meet the delightful Sir Tom.

And there was a sequel to the Sandy Thomson phone-call on Grampian's 1978 Hogmanay show. Many years later at a reception following the stage show at the Assembly Rooms, Wick, one of the organising officials tapped me on the shoulder to say that a gentleman by the name of Sandy Webster would like to meet me. I was duly led to an elderly presence and had some difficulty – partly because of the complicated nature of the story and partly because of Sandy's strange accent, an amalgam of local Caithness and Aberdeenshire Doric – in understanding what he was trying to tell me. Maybe at that stage in the evening I had had a glass or two myself, but with the help of Mrs Webster, the blind leading the blind finally made the breakthrough.

The day after that Hogmanay broadcast in the course of which Sandy Thomson had been phoning the Queen, Sandy Webster, going about his business in the streets of Wick, kept being button-holed by people. "Heard yer name on the TV last night, Sandy," they would say, and the reason he wanted to meet me was to find out why, in the character of Sandy Thomson, I had mentioned not only his name but where he came from,

---

[1] Actually Tom's persona was not merely noble – it was biblical. After all he had played Jesus of Nazareth on black and white television in the Fifties.

which was the Castle of Mey where he and Mrs Webster were the permanent staff.

Gradually, very gradually, it dawned that there is a wee sequence in the phone-call to the Queen where the name Sandy Webster crops up.

"Oh yes, your Majesty, you and I have met," Sandy Thomson says. "You maybe winna mind me, but I mind you. It was 1954, I think it wis… Ballater Station… Guard of Honour… 4th/7th Gordon Highlanders… I wis second frae the left in the middle row, atween Colour Sergeant McLeod and Sandy Webster. Eh? Fit's that? Aye, Sandy's fine. He's still the Stationmaster at Cambus o'May … Eh? God, is that a fact? Weel, naebody's never telt Sandy aboot it being closed doon."

Now this is a good example of people hearing what they want to hear. In this case some people in Wick wanted to hear me, in the course of my imaginary Sandy Thomson phone-call, make a real and factual association between their kenspeckle local Sandy Webster and nearby Castle of Mey, not Cambus o'May, a tiny area of Deeside they'd never heard of, and the stamping ground of another imaginary Sandy – Webster this time. Yes – it is confusing, isn't it?

It was a pity to have to disappoint Mr and Mrs Webster, but I was soon forgiven, introductions were made to George and Buff and in no time at all we were being invited to pay a visit to the famous Castle of Mey. We did so next day and as well as being given the privilege of a private tour (much faded grandeur – more faded than grand) we were treated by Mrs Webster to a pretty special afternoon tea – on a par I would say, with the one you get in the pavilion at the Oldmeldrum Sports (See Chapter 14). Maybe Sandy Thomson is due the Queen another phone-call on the following lines.

"Is that you, yer Majesty? I'm jist gie'in' ye a phonie tae thank ye very much for botherin' tae spik tae me. I'm really obliged tae ye because the rare blethers we've had have been responsible for a puckly good things that have happened tae me, includin' a lot o' laughs and twa o' the grandest afternoon teas ye could think o' – fit treats they've been – the best teas I have had in my life."

The other and greater disappointment was to do with the BBC Comedy Unit, set up, as I recall, in Glasgow in the early Eighties on the initiative of Pat Chalmers, Controller of BBC Scotland. Responsible for many good things at BBC Scotland, Pat was an admirer of the landmark BBC1 show *Not the Nine o' Clock News* and persuaded two of its key people, Colin Gilbert and Sean Hardie, to come up to Scotland with a free hand to do their own thing. So the Comedy Unit was established and its first venture was actually in radio, when I got the call to take part in a series called *Naked Radio,* my fellow performers being Tony Roper, Marcella Evaristi and Ron Bain, under the direction of Colin Gilbert and Tom Kininmont. Another well-known name who was involved in the early stages was the late Tom McGrath who, for whatever reason I know not, didn't stay on until the actual broadcasts.

Although I didn't continue into a second series either, I must have remained sufficiently *persona grata* with Colin for him and Sean Hardie to commission Buff and me to write a trial first episode for a television situation comedy which we had put up for consideration, with a working title *The Italians.* We really did love the idea and the comic possibilities of an Italian immigrant family now in their second, third and fourth generations living and working in a small Scottish town, and we did a lot of work on the project. Alas, it was not to be. It was eventually turned down or allowed to run into the sand. The comedy series which did go out under the Comedy Unit banner was *City Lights.* The fact that this was both Glasgow- and studio-based maybe told against us for reasons of economy and scale, but better to have tried and enjoyed the experience before falling short, than never to have made the effort at all.

As it happened there was an interesting sequel to our disappointment. Perhaps by way of compensation, a year or two later the Comedy Unit got back in touch and offered me a small cameo part in an episode of *City Lights.* The timing was perfect, because we were to be in Glasgow doing our new show at the King's, and rehearsal and recording could easily be fitted in during the day. I therefore accepted and spent an enjoyable time at the Queen Margaret Drive Studios with a cheery young cast who were beginning to make big names for themselves, including Gerard Kelly, Andy Gray, Jonathan Watson, Elaine C. Smith and David Anderson. Well, maybe the last two weren't quite so young, but they were a lot younger than I was and although they were all very welcoming I did feel a bit of an in-aboot comer to this close-knit jolly crew, an alien outsider. And an ancient one at that, who didn't get asked again…

Consolation came in a strange way. I had chanced to buy a *Scotsman* on the way to rehearsal one morning and, while waiting for the director Ron Bain to decide something, I came upon, surprise, oh happy surprise, a review of STW? at the King's a couple nights before.

I could scarcely believe that there was such a review, since *The Scotsman* is an Edinburgh paper and this was Glasgow we were in, and also because it was such a complimentary piece. The writer's name was Joseph Farrell and he could hardly have been more glowing in his praise. Modesty and a bad memory prevent me...etc...etc... but the point of this story is that, much as I would have wanted to interrupt my nice young fellow actors who were no doubt jabbering away, laughing and joking at the latest bit of showbiz gossip, exclaiming to them, "Here, look at this, you guys. How's that for a crit?" I just could not do it. I stayed mum, quietly hugging myself. And why? I still don't know. Many years later, writing this book and recalling the incident for Eva, she said, "Well, you're very modest you know," and then added, "with a lot to be modest about".

To which I replied, "Yes...I suppose so. And I'm very proud of my modesty". To which she replied, "Yes, and you're very modest about your pride".

22. STW? and our Records, Cassettes, CDs, Videos and DVDs

> "Ye'll never believe this but I have still got
> some o' yer aul vinyl records."
> – Anonymous gentleman, at a recent reception

I t is always nice to get that sort of unsolicited remark and my usual response these days is along the lines, "My goodness – you must be much older than you look." Which was probably quite true in the above case, considering that our first vinyl effort came out in 1973 following our elevation to the grandeur of HMT when it seemed, in current parlance, a no-brainer if we didn't make a recording of what we had done and then produce an L.P.

"The black one," we called it in later years to distinguish it from the other ten which eventually emerged, and the combined forces of the whole STW? family, kids as well, scrabbling about on our living-room floor, were required to get a single vinyl disc into a single glossy sleeve.

And then another, and another amid much jollification until there was a production line going, the technical boss of which was above such menial activity. This was a highly-skilled backroom boffin, Ron Miller by name, optician by profession, recording and film expert by inclination.

Ron had been brought in to help by James, and he was invaluable to us from our very first visit to HMT, right up to the time of his untimely death. He was a quiet, reserved man, much happier in the private world of his home cinema than in the company of a lot of people. I suspect that as well as respecting him and appreciating what he did for us, we also liked him more than he liked us, we who must have been too extrovert and arty-craftyish for his subdued and rather nervous taste.

Always a mile behind the times in relation to matters technological, it is likely that, at the time of producing our first vinyl record (at least it was not the 10-inch bakelite which I remember so well) we should have been bringing out a cassette. By the time we got round to these, the rest of the world had moved on to CDs. And now that, in our retirement, we've got round to doing a couple of 'Best of' CDs we hear words like 'I-pods' and 'Blackberries' and 'downloading' bandied about; all, we are told, to do with listening to recorded material – on your own, in private. Sounds unhealthy to me. And awfully complicated. I cannot see STW? going down any more recording roads. But you never know.

Although Buff and I share a deep suspicion of anything electronic, George has always loved gadgets and gizmos. Even when we were away doing a one-night engagement somewhere, George would disappear in search of a new toaster or a fancy coffee-making machine. As his late mother-in-law, a charming French lady, used to remark of him, "Ah Georges…he ees always worshipping false gods".

LPs or cassettes, they did well enough through the Seventies for us to win an award – exactly for what I don't remember (last-ever use of vinyl, perhaps?) – but it certainly entailed a trip to Glasgow and the Albany Hotel early in 1980 for a splendid evening in starry company including Andy Stewart and Lena Zavarone. The ceremony was called the Scotstar Awards and it was clearly a public relations affair of a most generous kind by a wholesale family business with a big interest in selling recorded material. We met some members of the extended family and were made welcome guests in their own home next day, so we formed a very favourable impression of the event.

It was also a pleasure, although secretly an embarrassment, to meet Andy Stewart for the first time. I could not help but be aware as we were making small talk about his hideaway home near Lumphanan, a part of Aberdeenshire I know well, that this very nice man had been the object of some pretty robust micky-taking from STW? over the last decade and

Last of the vinyl records.

PHOTO: ABERDEEN JOURNALS

more. Did he know that one of our most successful numbers was a take-off of his most successful number and that I had been impersonating him? And if he did know, did he mind? Or, hopefully, was he flattered? Although our paths crossed a few times after that, I never found out, and Andy died, far too young, in 1993.

Many years later I met up with an old school friend, Jimmy Reith, and in the course of our catch-up it emerged that he had known Andy well when they had been students together at the Royal Scottish Academy of Music and Drama. In fact they had shared digs on Glasgow's Southside; they had even shared a room, so Jimmy got to know Andy really well and was full of admiration for the talent he was showing even then and which, in that earlier chapter, I touched on fleetingly. Far too fleetingly.

Jimmy spoke of Andy's improvisations – conversations conjured up among real or imaginary characters and he remembered particularly trying to get to sleep one night while Andy from his bed at the other side of the room conducted a three-way conversation between Winston Churchill, Humphrey Bogart and Field-Marshall Rommel. He doesn't remember how it ended but, more than fifty years later, cannot forget how it began.

"It is not often," declaimed Churchill breaking the silence of the pitch-black bedroom, "that I have been asked to decorate an enemy general…"

"Now, now Winston," lisped Bogart, "he ain't a general, he's an effing Field-Marshall…" at which Jimmy could not contain his laughter and, thus encouraged, Andy knew he had engaged his audience and launched further into his flight of comic fantasy. As Jimmy said, "I told him he was not a singer – I had got fed up hearing him in the shower bawling out Gluck's great aria *Che-faro Senza Eurydice* – and to stick to comedy at which he was brilliant."

Well, as we all know, he stuck to both and the irony is that it is the singing of a different kind which brought him greatest popular success and by which he is best remembered, since there is surely not a CD stack at any filling-station or general shoppie in any tiny village in the land which doesn't feature something of Andy in proud Caledonian mode. And yet that's not the whole story. Into the songs went the same kind of creativity as informed his less well-remembered comedy. As well as being a performer, he had a real talent for what my friend Jimmy called his "improvisations" which were the result of a very fertile mind buzzing with ideas, both comic and serious. Television and the tartan image concealed far greater capabilities and it was a pity that as the years rolled on he didn't change the emphasis of his working life.

A tiny but sad example of the time-warp in which he got stuck comes to mind; STW? followed him and his company into the King's in Edinburgh one year and there, still pinned to a wall in the wings was the running-order of his show a day or two before. It seemed as tired and tatty as the scrap of paper on which it had been scribbled. And it needn't have been, and why was it so? If, as Andy did, you have the timing and voices for comedy as a performer, you can pretty comfortably change to acting. Usually anyway, I suggest. I can think of any number of comedians who have become accomplished actors, but few great actors who are much good at comedy. Anyway, Andy had already established his credentials as an actor, Jimmy told me, having won an important prize at the RSAMD for his stunning portrayal of a French waiter wearing, as Jimmy was amused to boast, a pair of his gold cufflinks.

So why didn't Andy make the gradual move into the legitimate side of the entertainment business? Pride? Fear of the unknown? Frequent bouts of illness? Lack of honest professional advice? Maybe this last possibility did have a lot to do with it because his close associate – manager, minder, stage feed and factotum Max Kaye – emigrated to Perth, Western Australia, which he'd fallen in love with when touring with Andy. He's still there after twenty-five happy and successful years, but it is a sad irony that while he was prospering, Andy was in deep decline.

Max and his wife Norma, a fine dancer in her day, entertained Eva and myself to lunch at his club a few years ago when we were in Perth visiting our son Stephen. A natural turn of the conversation took us to his long connection with Andy. "We were like brothers," said Max and I believed him. There was real affection and regret in the voice and Norma nodded in agreement.

There is one last story about Andy Stewart, from Jimmy Reith, that is worth the telling. Along the coast out of Arbroath where Andy was brought up, there is a deep, dark cave well-known for its properties of dramatic resonance. Andy had been stravaiging out and about one day and fetched up away at the back of it when a party of visitors arrived to test it out.

"Hello there," one called out resoundingly from the entrance.

"Hello there," echoed Andy in a ghostly voice from the gloom.

"Hello again," cried the visitor. And again came the spooky echo,

"Hello again."

There were one or two more "Hellos" and then the visitor called, "What are you doing?"

And back came the scary reply, "I am having a pee"...which description of the bodily function owes more to politeness than accuracy, but certainly underlines Andy's sense of humour.

This revisionist take on a more important figure in Scotland's culture than would probably be acknowledged in snootier circles is maybe some sort of small payback for all the fun and laughter STW? enjoyed at Andy's expense over many, many years. If our proposed TV situation comedy series *The Italians* had come to fruition, and if I had had anything to do with it, Andy would certainly have been invited to play one of the main parts.

23. STW? and Our Two Books
Sketches and Songs 1987
and Second Helping 1996

**"Did you ever think about STW? doing a book?
'Cos I think you should."**
– Gordon Wright,
Edinburgh publisher and book-lover, photographer and jazz-lover,
bachelor finally turned husband, and Carmen and Robbie-lover,
one of Nature's really good guys

I need hardly say more but I will. The above quote was directed at me in my dressing-room at the King's, Glasgow, in 1985. The speaker who had gained admittance to all of us separately in turn was a tall, bald, bespectacled chap who came quickly to the point – which was swiftly and adroitly swatted away by all of us on the honest grounds that, being a democratic organisation, we had to meet together to discuss the matter before a decision could be made.

Which didn't take very long since Gordon's credentials and personality were, democratically speaking, easy to approve; and we had nothing to lose. Not financially anyway, although we were to find that there was quite a bit of time and effort involved in getting a book – any kind of book – into print. And in the beginning we didn't even know what kind of book we wanted. I think there was a vague idea that each of us might write in his own way about his own contribution, but for various reasons that proved impracticable. It might have been Gordon himself (or maybe James?) who declared firmly that the best idea was simply to reproduce the scripts, music and lyrics which seemed to have gone down well with the public. What was more, Gordon was prepared to transpose these from the records and cassettes – a job he attacked on his own with due efficiency.

Not so speedy was the progress thereafter when the partners of STW? had to become involved. None of us – except James – was very quick at doing things and coping with the exploration of new territory – such minefields as proof-reading, layouts, captions, credits, music transcription and photo selection – were a slow process for us, even with Gordon's expert help. Buff and I as writers succumbed to the temptation of doing footnotes for most of the sketches and lyrics. That was fun when we started – it may well be that the reader was not too impressed by some pretty corny stuff when the book came out – but we enjoyed doing them, although as time went on we realised we had made a rod for our own backs and such phrases as "bloody bind" and "what a chore" just might have crept into the vocabulary.

Never mind, we got there, and struggled through our steep learning curve thanks to Gordon's patient support, which didn't stop at publication. As a one-man business Gordon had to be a salesman as well and we were happy to comply with his request to do various book launches and signings. Although the thoughts in writing the foregoing related to our first book ("the yellow one" we came to call it on account of the colour of the cover) they would as easily apply to the second ("the blue one") with the qualification that, having been over the course before, we didn't find it so difficult second time round.

It was just a pity that after the relative success of the yellow one, the blue one didn't do well at all, due in all probability to the delay in publication, certainly no fault of Gordon who suffered financially as a result. Instead of the book coming out to coincide with the end of our farewell tour *Final Fling* at HMT in November 1995, or even at Christmas that year when STW? was very high profile, it didn't appear until Christmas 1996 by which time we were long retired and the public weren't interested in yesterday's news. The pity is that the blue one is actually that bit better, in my opinion, more professional and accomplished, than the yellow one.

Looking for inspiration for the two books

This branch of the STW? Cottage Industry will not be complete without further reference to our great friend Gordon. "Great" certainly. But also – and I write this in warmth and affection – also geeky and, dare I say it, goofy? That's an exaggeration due to the cheap temptation of alliteration, but it is fair to say that this son of Aul' Reekie – who took the initiative long years ago of getting his fellow citizen and former pupil of Darroch Secondary School, Sean Connery, to join his local branch of the SNP – <u>is</u> a character, a 'one off.'

Gordon was all of the bits of that description, but what we responded to more than anything was that he was extremely amusing – in several senses. Firstly and secondly and thirdly he told a good story against himself. In his self-deprecating way he always seemed to be the accident-prone victim of circumstance, most notably when he went to Rumania to get married to Carmen and encountered difficulties of language, religious custom and bureaucracy. As he scoffed his jumbo fish and chips, or jam roly-poly and custard – most of our social exchanges with Gordon involved large quantities of food not all of which reached its intended destination – his anecdotal skill and gossipy knowledge of the Edinburgh scene made him great company. It came as no surprise to learn that he had written material for certain well-known stand-up comedians.

His sense of humour and his way with words and print technology manifested themselves when we would all of us be the recipients of occasional spoof letters, such as the one I received from Buckingham Palace purporting to have been written by Prince Charles:

Buckingham Palace
18 July 1986

Dear Stephen,

How are you? I hear you are all having a marvellous success with your new show. How wonderful. As you probably know, they have adapted my story 'The Old Man of Lochnagar' for the stage and it will be presented at His Majesty's later this year. It is all very confusing being involved in show business for the first time and I was wondering if you could give me a few pointers. For instance, how on earth do you manage to get your pictures in the papers so often? Does this mean a lot of back-handers to the Press? I really don't know how I am going to cope when I am expected to look after the kids, find a stripper for Andrew's stag night and prepare for another world tour. However, I am intent on doing my best to help promote the show and this means keeping in touch with all that's happening in Grampian. We've an awful job getting the P&J down here. W. H. Smith across the road are always four days behind with delivery. In fact, if they don't get their fingers out soon, that 'by Appointment' sign's coming down. Is there any chance you could bum a copy of 'Far's the Paper' from Buff for me? I am looking for something suitable for Granny's birthday and the 'Francis Gay Friendship Book' is up to £2.95 this year. By the way, I should tell you that Granny is one of your biggest fans and your records are never off her gramophone. She loves playing them to friends and visiting dignitaries, especially the one where she is referred to by 'the Moderator'. My God! She fairly bored the arse off Kenneth Kaunda the last time he was in for his tea. To give him his due, he sat bleary-eyed through 'Scotland the What at Home', 'More Scotland the What' and 'Back at His Majesty's' before he finally nodded off and fell off the end of the settee. The Queen was very upset when she heard and is going to have a word with her. Granny's lack of interest in the state of emergency in S.A. is a bit disappointing. Her world seems to revolve round 'The Sunday Post', your records and Campbell's Cream of Tomato Soup these days. Come to think of it, President Kaunda didn't like the soup either.

I should also mention that our head gardener at the Palace is from Aberdeen. He worked on the Balmoral Estate before we managed to entice him down to London in 1979. Archie is an absolute wizard with roses and privet hedging and has enhanced the grounds considerably since his arrival. He is quite a favourite with the rest of the staff who are often amused by his broad Scots tongue. Every time he discovers one of Auntie Margaret's dead gin bottles concealed in a privet he comes out with words like 'Fitafaksis'. Words none of us understand.

I suppose we will all be at Braemar for the games this year. All that heather fairly goes for Diana's sinuses and these clegs are a bugger when they get up your kilt. Farquharson of Invercauld says he can get a man called Barron to walk up and down in front of the Royal pavilion with an insecticide spray for only a fiver. Might be worthy the money if Farquharson's paying.

I hear you are taking the show on to Edinburgh for the Festival this year. It really is a terrible job getting accommodation in Edinburgh during the Festival, so if you are stuck, see Col. McIver at Holyroodhouse and tell him I said was it would be alright for you to have Mary Queen of Scot's bed. They'll divert the tourists through Rizzio's room and let you get your sleep in the afternoon.

I do hope you will all be able to come and see our little effort when it opens in Aberdeen. The tickets will all be very reasonably priced.

Kind Regards,
Charles

Thank you, Gordon, for enriching our lives, if not our pockets.

Part Five

STW? and Special Events

Preface

The last part of this book is to do with mopping up. If that sounds like I am about to write a lot of rubbish, so be it. I accept that the law of unintended consequence may well come into play, but the aim is to look at as many subjects as I think are worth a chapter or so, however brief, and which haven't been covered already.

So here goes, and I cannot think of a better way to do it than in chronological order.

24. Royal Scottish Variety Performance
2nd October 1983

"Princess Diana? What a job I have had getting
through to you. Does yer mither-in-law ken that
she's nae in the book? I tried under Q, I tried under ER,
then I tried under Balmoral and I got a boarding-house
in Great Western Road, Aiberdeen..."

Having performed what came to be known as 'the futret phone-call' at the re-opening of HMT the year before, it was natural to do it again when STW? was invited to participate in the Royal Scottish Variety Performance "in the presence of Their Royal Highnesses the Prince and Princess of Wales at the King's Theatre, Glasgow."

After all, Charles had heard the piece and seemed to have liked it, so the hope was that Diana would too. Whether she did or not I do not know, because when I was presented momentarily after the show I did not ask and she did not say. I was too busy preventing my jaw from dropping at her stunning presence and then eavesdropping on the exchange she had with Andy Cameron, who was standing next to me in the line-up.[1]

The whole affair was produced at short notice by the great Jimmy Logan following the sudden death of the original choice, Ian McFadyen of BBC Scotland Television, and a fine job he made of it. Jimmy even managed to participate himself with the equally marvellous Rikki Fulton in a well-known, well-worked sketch involving a ladder going up to the royal box. Conspicuous by his absence from what appeared to be a cast of thousands judging by the crammed dressing-rooms, stage and wings, was Andy Stewart, (did he provide a sickness note, was he touring, or was his omission in some way political?); but apart from Andy, just about everybody in Scotland who had ever trod a professional board seemed to be there, including one or two who must have been let out of an old folks' home for the night, and a few guitar twangers who had surely escaped from youth custody.

We bumped into the singing solicitor Peter Morrison quite a lot and came to share with him an interest not only in the translation, but also the pronunciation of a Latin phrase or two from a song which was not in his usual repertoire. The words *alere flammam* (to feed the flame) come to mind, part of the anthem of a Glasgow secondary school called Bellahouston Academy of which Jimmy was a former pupil, and he had chosen it as a chorus number to close the show.

Quite why we never knew − nor did Peter − and we rather doubted if anybody else did, so it was an odd feeling to be joining in, contributing to the joyful noise of a stageful of strangers, with heartiness and seeming comprehension when we had not the foggiest notion of what it was all about.

Of that huge company of artistes I don't remember everyone and the

---

[1] I should explain that the purpose of the evening was to raise the awareness of − and funds for − a hospice for the terminally ill. The hospice had been presented by Glasgow District Council to a Trust established to hold and own the property, a fine terraced block of outstanding architectural quality. For the best of all charitable reasons the Council and the Trust decided that the property would be named The Prince and Princess of Wales Hospice and would be dedicated to their Royal Highnesses as the city of Glasgow's wedding gift. And a most ingenious wedding gift it was − ensuring that the wonderful couple would be obliged to take more than a passing interest in the project for the benefit of its fund-raising activities.

Anyway, there we were in the line-up, STW? and Andy Cameron, and I could not help overhearing the following exchange as Princess Diana towered elegantly above him:

"Did ye like yer weddin' present, Ma'am?"

"Well, it is most unusual…"

"Aye, it is no' the kinda thing ye can pit in yer bottom drawer."

(There's no answer to that and HRH drifted on graciously)

programme is lost, but others I do recall included Jimmy's sister Annie Ross, Kenneth McKellar, Helen McArthur, Hector Nicol, Bill McCue, Dougie Donnelly and Chic Murray. Or was Chic there? Must have been. An evening like that could not have taken place without Chic, surely.

Afterthought... After the parting of the ways for Charles and Diana, I wonder what the hospice is called now?

25. The London Visits

**"How lovely to see you again and I gather that was
a very funny show."**
**– Green room greeting from very charming,
very Home Counties lady after our show in the
Queen Elizabeth Hall, South Bank**

The first time STW? went to London was in 1978 at the invitation of the Aberdeen University Club's local branch – and I am quite prepared to argue that there is nowhere more local, indeed parochial in outlook, than London. By the time we arrived in London again in 1985 we had gone fully professional and were there under our own steam, admittedly with quite a bit of help from two gentlemen who had been cleverly enlisted by James.

The first of these was Antony Phillips, who had moved on to an important administrative job on the South Bank, and he it was who got us installed for three nights in the Queen Elizabeth Hall. Antony rather approved of the approach we had taken to winkling out our most likely audience.

This was a circular letter addressed, after considerable homework, to as many old friends, acquaintances and Scots-related organisations as we could think of, and it read as follows:

Scotland the What?
c/o Queen Elizabeth Hall
South Bank
London

Dear Scottish Exile

You may already have heard of our show 'Scotland the What?' More probably the name will mean nothing to the London Scot long exiled from the cool culture of the North to the outback of Belgravia or the steaming jungles of Wimbledon. Such ignorance is entirely forgiveable since the furthest we have so far ventured has been the Theatre Royal, Dumfries, just on the edge of civilization as we know it. Perilous days lie ahead of us, since we are about to undertake our first expedition to the London stage, unknown territory which we fear we may find altogether too barren without a little help from kith and kin. Hence this letter with which we offer, firstly, an apology for leaning over-heavily on our shared ethnic origins and, secondly, the accompanying brochure and booking slip which we would devoutly pray you to complete in the cause of Presbyterian solidarity and to save us from losing our shirts.

Actually we suspect you might have rather an enjoyable evening. We put it no more strongly because of that native modesty which, as a fellow Scot, you will know is really just a fear of tempting fate, but which does permit us a casual nod in the direction of our track record, detailed in purple prose in the brochure. It is this dizzy progress which has precipitated us recklessly into full-time show business after only umpteen years' indulgence in Scotland the What? as a hobby. There may have been more unusual symptoms of the male menopause but few so eccentric and none which has provided such innocent amusement, at least to the participants.

A final word: one of the nice things about taking the show around the country is that old friends and acquaintances appear in unlikely places after an embarrassing number of years. London should be fertile ground for a bit of serendipity and nostalgia encouraged by a well-stocked Green Room. So if you happened to know us in the dim and distant past, please do not hesitate to come round for a quick glass of lemonade.

We hope you come to see us.

Yours sincerely,
Buff Hardie, George Donald, Stephen Robertson, James Logan,
known collectively as Scotland the What?

...following which effort we did get great audiences – ninety per cent exiles as expected, and as warm, appreciative and friendly as we had ever experienced before.

The other angel of mercy who used his contacts to render a high-class concert hall fit for staging a theatrical event was a real, genuine, copper-bottomed impresario called Robert Luff, a most interesting man who died in 2009 in his nineties. I still do not know how James organised this. Robert's obituary in the national broadsheets told us far more about him – producer, agent, multiple theatre owner, ex-soldier, philanthropist – than we had ever known, which was simply that he was a most agreeable, conventionally suited, conventionally bald old buffer, a little lonely perhaps, who was delighted to accept our invitation to supper after the show. This was at an Italian restaurant, Bertorelli's, well-known in its day, opposite the stage-door of the Royal Opera House, Covent Garden – and we celebrated not only the success of our venture, but also Buff's fifty-fourth birthday on the fourth of January. There was just one fly in the ointment.

Happy birthday, Buff. Robert Luff in party mode.

The show had been an undoubted success, socially as well as theatrically, as the following piece from *The Press & Journal* was generous enough to confirm, but there was little monetary gain due to the presence of the four wives who made it their business to make huge savings at London's January Sales.

Here is the P&J report:

Scotland the What? team conquers London
Theatre, by Brian Taylor

It was probably a bit like Wembley. All you can hear are Scottish voices but you know there must be Sassenachs in there somewhere.

In truth the audience for the performance of Scotland the What? in London might have provided some rich material for a new skit by the North-East comic trio.

For these were the born-again Aberdonians. The accents in the bar over the interval whisky were just a little too determinedly Scottish, the reminiscences – "It's fine to hear the auld tongue again" – just a fraction too sentimental to accord with the often biting satire of the performance.

It was Hugh McDiarmid who wrote of "Crouse London Scotties wi' their braw shirt fronts". They were out in force at the Queen Elizabeth Hall in the South Bank arts complex.

This view is of course far too caustic. The audiences – not far from capacity over the three nights up to Saturday – enjoyed themselves thoroughly and the venture was pronounced a success by the performers and their director James Logan who had voiced his usual pessimism in advance.

Of course the trio had the exiled Aberdonians on their side from the start. Placenames were cheered.

Stephen Robertson had but to mention Rhynie – the starting point of so many of his sketches – to win an appreciative murmur. And the audience positively hooted in approval when famous Aberdeen sites were brought into the programme.

As a London Scot myself I decided in the interests of accuracy to conduct an in-depth survey of English reaction to the show.

Both of them confessed that they had not understood every section – perhaps Mr Robertson's comical criticism of North-East agricultural communities left them a little in the dark – but they had acknowledged real comic brilliance, warmed to the musical talent of George Donald and found the entire affair "a lot of fun".

Significantly, they reserved most of their praise for the satirical sections which are the base of the show: the public official on the make, the send-ups of tartan-clad performers, the jibes at less endearing Scottish characteristics, above all, the mockery of English-educated Scots trying to revive a culture which is alien to them.

It has always seemed to me that Scotland the What? get away with the most outrageous satire and hard-hitting comment because it is overlaid with real humour, warmth, and sheer skill in stagecraft. And of course, they are Aberdonians reflecting satirically on their own.

One of the sketches in the London show cast Buff Hardie as a dour Aberdonian giving a cold response to a typically effervescent American who had sought him out with news of a trans-Atlantic relation.

The audience roared with laughter. If an Englishman had dared to suggest that Aberdonians ever behaved in such an inhospitable fashion…

But Scotland the What? have always been beautifully in tune with their audience, especially in the North-East – even when their humour was directed at the audience themselves.

The lawyer, teacher and health service administrator turned comedians have often exactly matched the root feeling of the audience about an issue.

I still remember the encouraging roar which greeted a satirical reflection on plans to develop much of central Aberdeen.

The London shows – in an elegant concert hall usually devoted to classical music – combine satire on new events with old favourites from past shows. I am reliably informed that only six words were Anglicized in the interests of international relations.

It seems likely that the lads may look further afield now. A visit to Australia could be on the cards and the prospect of tapping Caledonian spirit in Canada has also been mentioned.

But the show, thankfully, remains Aberdeen-rooted: and the London programme even credited the assistance of "The Press & Journal" and its Editor Peter Watson, along with other Aberdeen organizations including, of course, HM Theatre, the home ground.

The back stage party on Saturday night was, therefore, a time for celebration of a victory before the long theatrical trail North via Dunfermline to Inverurie.

But, in true fashion, the hospitality had to end at 11.15pm. After that time, a surcharge was applied.

– *The Press & Journal, January 1985*

Presumably Peter Watson, Editor of the P&J at the time and a canny Aberdonian to his securely grounded feet, considered all that praise too fulsome by half and made sure that Brian Taylor was never given such extravagant rope again. The poor chap left print journalism and absconded to the telly and BBC Scotland where he is now Political Editor. You cannot miss him. He has so bloomed over the years that his physical presence matches the purple prose. How long can the psychedelic galluses stand the strain? As long as humanly possible, please – I wouldn't want any harm to come to a broadcaster who did wonders for STW?'s credibility. All these years later he has succeeded in inducing such vanity in your author as to cause him to look out this superlative piece of prose. A bit embarrassing, though, I must admit. And we never did get to Australia or Canada.

"Sorry, Principal, I canna afford tae gie ye mair than a couple o' million."

PHOTO: ABERDEEN JOURNALS

1987: We returned to London a couple of years later, the kind of gap we liked to leave between visits, and this time our choice of venue was The Bloomsbury Theatre, part of London University. We did a week there and again things went pretty well, the social scene enlivened by back-stage visits from old friends, and lunch invitations, including to one of the Clydesdale Banks, Courtesy of our local MP, Frank Doran, we also visited the one and only House of Commons where we had the privilege of being insulted by a well-refreshed John Prescott.

The Bloomsbury engagement was the last of our autumn season and at the end of it we broke up and left in different directions, Eva and I to go to Cyprus for a well-earned holiday before the rigours of a family Christmas. It was only when we got home that we learned the bad news that the big trunk containing all our props, which had been left in the temporary care of the Bloomsbury staff, had gone missing, presumably stolen. But who could have done that? Well I did say that the Bloomsbury was part of the local university and where there are students there are high jinks and goodness knows what other irresponsible goings-on, stretching probably to petty theft. We will never know, and though the tatty props were no great loss, another item in the trunk most assuredly was. This was the complete list of all our London contacts, absolutely essential for any future visit and impossible to replace without repeating all that rigmarole of research and homework of two or three years previously.

And so, lacking the energy and democratic will, STW? didn't go to London again,[1] never mind Australia or Canada.

[1] Actually, that is not completely true... Certainly, we did not return with the show but we did find ourselves recruited by Aberdeen University to help with their Quincentenary celebrations and, among other venues, enjoyed helping to entertain London exiles at Lancaster House where George played classily and Buff and I performed a sketch in which he played the Principal and I played a wealthy farmer.

26. Back to the Edinburgh Festival

"Quite a nice invitation today, lads. Frank Dunlop would like us to do a show at the Festival"
— James Logan at coffee one morning, early 1986

Frank Dunlop was not who Buff thought he was to begin with. A diehard supporter of Aberdeen Football Club all his life, Buff could never forget Frank Dunlop as the captain and centre-half of the Dons, who held the trophy aloft when they won the Scottish Cup in 1947. At what stage in the intervening thirty-nine years had this hero of his boyhood made the move from the round ball game to the more effete field of the Arts. And why? There had been nothing about such an unusual change of career in the P&J, either in its numerous sporting pages at the back, or in the odd half-column allocated to culture somewhere in the middle...at the bottom of the page...on a Tuesday...every second week...or was it third?

All right, the joke has been milked enough and indeed Buff would have been one of the few people in the world who would have known about both Frank Dunlops (no known relationship); the one who was the footballer of a bygone age and the other who was the Director of the Edinburgh Festival. Now that's the official Edinburgh Festival we're talking about, not all that Fringe rubbish where we had started out seventeen years before.

It really was a feather in our now quite elderly caps (and not just in revue terms) to get an invitation like this. And we jumped at it – jumped, that is, in our terms. That means to say our democratic process speeded up to the point at a partners' meeting where the wives hardly yawned at all. Frank (sounds a bit too familiar but, hell, this is real show business we're talking now, where name-dropping is obligatory) – Frank booked us in to the Royal Lyceum to do five late-night shows to follow such heavier offerings as the London Festival Ballet, the Market Theatre of Johannesburg, a couple of Spanish dramas by Lorca and a French job by God knows who. This was international culture of the most serious kind, great for minority interests, but not significant opposition in popular box-office terms. Not too surprising, then, that we were booked out before we ever got to Edinburgh, a happy situation which led to some smugness on my part, I must confess.

A lady of my acquaintance, something of a culture vulture, had spotted STW?'s inclusion in the Festival Diary with ill-concealed surprise.

"My goodness! How are you going to get on?" she enquired. "The main Festival will be quite a challenge."

"Och, I think we should be OK," I replied. "Anyway, we're booked out in advance, so we're not too worried."

What a boaster! I reflected later that I should have been more modest about my pride, or a bit prouder of my modesty. As it happened, we didn't need to be worried at all. Although this was the first time we had appeared at the Lyceum – and before its renovation our impression of the theatre, particularly back-stage and the one ropy dressing-room which we had been allocated, had not been too favourable – we had, much more importantly, begun to establish quite a strong foothold on the Edinburgh scene.

We were now regular visitors to the King's, building up from one week to three weeks there under the encouraging management of Chris Potter whom we had previously known at the Adam Smith, Kirkcaldy, and our acceptance by a traditionally reserved public was reflected also by the generous private hospitality we were privileged to be receiving.

This all took place over several visits, of course, not just in the week of the 1986 Festival, but even in that limited period there were examples of our rising status. These had both to do with *The Scotsman* which had been so supportive of us from the beginning; the first was a decent review, not from any of the usual Festival stringers, but by the finance and economics

Cue for a queue   PHOTO: GORDON WRIGHT

writer Peter Jones. This we took as a compliment on the grounds that it was only right and fitting that gentlemen of our experience and maturity should have the attention of the newspaper's heavier intelligentsia. The possibility that Peter was just helping out, having been drafted in and away from his normal patch because of Festival pressures, did not occur to us.

The other boost we got from *The Scotsman* began with a cheery phone call one morning from their Publicity Department, the manager no less, and a helluva decent sort at that, whom I had known and liked from away back in school and sporting days.

"Hello, Steve. Ian Thomson here…" he said and proceeded, after a laugh or two of well-remembered bonhomie, to invite STW? to come along to the Fringe Club and present The Scotsman Awards to various Fringe newcomers. This was a most generous gesture (or maybe Ian had not managed to get either of the Frank Dunlops and had had to resort to lesser fry) which we were very happy to accept. Although we didn't need the publicity for our own bookings, the photo of the ceremony which appeared in the paper next day[1] did no harm at all to our street cred and to the receipt of these rather pleasing invitations for private hospitality. Of which more anon…

---

[1] Looking at the scrapbook of the time, I see I am shaking hands with a youngster who was to become totally associated with the Fringe, and Artistic Director at the Assembly Rooms, William Burdett-Coutts.

... And anon could include 1990 which was the year we were again invited to take part in the official Festival. And this time we were back in the dear old King's. In the evening, that is. During the day we were very busy with our TV special as mentioned in Chapter 20. Not much time for socialising then, although I cannot possibly forget one very late night fetching up with John McLeod, the composer, as our guest in the Bar Roma at the West end of Princes Street when the first edition of the morning papers came out.

And once again *The Scotsman* turned up trumps for us. There we were, Buff, George and I – yes, we three, STW?, really were in a full-page photograph on the front of the special Festival supplement, in addition to which we discovered, as we nervously scanned the inside, a most enthusiastic review by Catherine Lockerbie. What a splendidly intelligent lady! It was quite a thrilling wee episode for us, rather improved by the irony that the item she had particularly enjoyed – one of my Doric phone-calls suitably adapted – we had already decided to cut on the grounds that it was too long and the show would benefit from being shortened. And though I cried into my Chianti we didn't go back on that and proceeded to have "what might be described as a not unsuccessful week", as John Major, Prime Minister at the time might have put it.

As for the hospitality, Edinburgh more than belied its reputation associated with the question, "You'll have had your tea?" As far as we were concerned, doors were flung open on our biennial visits to the King's and on quite a number of one-off occasions – so often that it is impossible to remember exactly when, but easy to remember by whom since without actually dropping names we were honoured to be the guests of a Moderator of the General Assembly, a Senator of the College of Justice, a GOC Scottish Command, not to mention the finest jazz musician in Scotland among lots of other weel and not-so-weel kent folk.

We were made to feel very much at home in Edinburgh and were even able to offer a bit of hospitality ourselves on occasion. Admittedly this tended to take the form of a slug of whisky in a grotty tumbler in one of our dressing-rooms when James would invite one of his Arts Council or Arts-related cronies or acquaintances to "come round".

One such guest was Sir Gerald Eliot, accompanied by his good lady, who was clearly dazzled by the back-stage glamour of mucky shirts chucked in the corner and the debris of discarded bunnets, bottles and make-up tat. Or was it Sir Alan and Lady Peacock who were thus mesmerised, all the while doing their well-mannered best – as we were – to conduct a conversation of meaningless banalities. Or was that Lady Havergel whom we had once known as Reg Barrett-Ayres' secretary and her stepson Giles of the Glasgow Citizen's? We even had the odd political visitor and were gratified that we found favour with both ends of the spectrum; Norman and Jenny Buchan on the left were well-known aficionados of the folk scene, and on the right Janet Buchanan-Smith, widow of Alick, accompanied by various family members, were just jolly good sorts.

From this wide range of well-wishers at the King's, my strongest image is of a lively face caught in the light at the end of the gloomy corridor leading to the ground floor dressing-rooms. A lively and familiar face. Such was the resemblance we had no need to be told we were to receive a call from the daughter of Harry Gordon – much better-looking than the great Aberdeen and Scottish comedian himself, but so like him in the pantomime dame role for which he was famous.

Actually I never saw Harry Gordon in that role, but remember him at HMT in the early Fifties in the *Five Past Eight* shows when his co-star was a youthful Jimmy Logan, his aged feed was Jack Holden and among the supporting cast was a promising young fella called Dickie Henderson. Dickie went on to become a big star in the West End and to have his own TV series, but, more importantly, married an Aberdeen graduate, Gwyneth Wycherly, a very pretty and talented girl who had been in the Students' Show with Buff and myself. Gwyneth, sadly, was widowed far too early, but got married happily a few years later to Dickie's best friend. I still see her occasionally if I happen to be in London.

But back to Bunty, Harry Gordon's daughter, who was at the King's with her husband to see their son who was in an administrative job there. I have to say – and time lends strength to the feeling – that there was something symbolic about meeting Bunty and shaking hands with her. She was after all the nearest and dearest link to Harry Gordon to whom STW? were privileged to be regarded, at least in North-East terms, as comedy's true heirs and successors.

As evidence of this entitlement and our appreciation of the connection there is a song called in Harry's day The Auldest Aberdonian which we adapted and updated in celebration of the much-loved comedy hero and which came to be more readily recognised by its chorus which began:

Fittie folk, Kitty folk, country folk and city folk,
Folk fae Constitution Street and folk fae Rubislaw Den,
Wallfield, Nellfield, Mannofield and Cattofield,
List to local stories that Professors dinna ken.

(Archie Hyslop's original last line)

Lots of local stories that ye'd maybe like tae ken.

(Our version of the last line)

Harry may have been the performer of the early version but the author of the words and music, whose nostalgic chorus remained very nearly intact when we restored the number, was a gentleman called Archibald Forbes Hyslop M.A., Ph.D. (1893-1943). He it was who wrote a lot of songs for Harry while pursuing a successful career in education, latterly as an Inspector of Schools in the Borders where he died just a few months after his late marriage to a girl twenty years younger than himself. This sad story of late romance was made even sadder by the fact that his widow lost a most gifted and extraordinary personality. Archie's life and his professional relationship with Harry Gordon would merit an interesting study, but suffice it here to say that I have been fortunate enough to track down a pretty substantial obituary in an old magazine of the Aberdeen Grammar School of which Archie like myself was a former pupil. Even allowing for the fulsome nature of prose nearly seventy years ago, it is clear that Archie was quite a guy. There are warm references to his human and academic qualities, but what concerns me are the talents which proved such a boon for Harry Gordon. Here are a couple of quotes:

"No-one who was associated with him … will ever forget the enormous fun which he distilled out of the various concerts, dramatic sketches and jamborees that he helped to run. On these occasions his bubbling humour, his brilliant gifts of histrionic and musical improvisation, his skill as a rhymester, his inexhaustible high spirits and unfailing zest… found their fullest scope."

"Many of the choruses which he composed and set to music will live imperishably in the memories of those who sang or heard them."

These words written so long ago ring remarkably true for STW?. As we traversed Scotland, pitching up more frequently than anywhere else at HMT between 1971 and 1995, *Fittie folk, Kitty folk* gradually morphed into the nearest we ever got to a signature tune. And although all the laughter came from the wit and topicality of Buff's new verses plus the occasional extra chorus, it was the warmth of that main chorus of Archie's infused by folk memory and community spirit which seemed to touch and unify our audiences and quite literally got their hands clapping. In time, too…

Two final points worth the telling: I was intrigued firstly to note that the obituary was subscribed by someone with the initials W.D.S., clearly a huge admirer of Archie and his junior by several years not just at school, but also in the Scouts which were at least one base for his blossoming theatrical talents.[2]

And it dawned on me only very slowly that W.D.S. stands for W. Douglas Simpson (1896-1968) the legendary librarian at Aberdeen University whom I well remember myself. And when I use the word 'legendary' I do so advisedly. He was the kind of considerable figure around whom colourful stories abounded, apocryphal or otherwise. And his daughter Anne remains a life-long friend of Isabelle Donald.

The last part of the story is that the Hyslop name survives in a collection of fine paintings in Aberdeen Art Gallery. After his death Archie's widow continued to live in their home in Melrose overlooking The Greenyards rugby field until her own death half a century later.

And it was at this point, the life-rent of her inheritance having expired, that the story entered the public domain that she had been occupying a virtual treasure-house of fine art. Archie had had a very good eye for pictures, particularly those of the Scottish Colourists which he had been able to buy mainly from the fees he had earned writing for Harry Gordon, and these had now been left in their entirety by Mrs Hyslop to Aberdeen Art Gallery in memory of her husband and his affection for his native city.

If then, dear reader, you find yourself strolling the balcony overlooking the atrium of that most splendid space and your eye is engaged by a Peploe – or Hunter or Cadell – think not only of its beauty, but of its provenance. It may be of passing interest, or even more serious contemplation, that its presence there is owed to the skill of Archie Hyslop's pen all these years

---

[2] Talking of the Scouts and theatrical talent I must take up that cue to pay tribute to an old pal who has been a force not just for good but for sterling excellence in both these areas of social activity. Graeme Wilson, business man for a living, combines both interests as a hobby. He was made M.B.E. for his services to Scouting a few years ago and for his interest and participation in, support of and contribution to both amateur and professional theatre, he has had for much longer and by popular acclaim a C.B.E. (Companion of Boundless Enthusiasm). He was also helluva generous to STW?.

ago. I don't think it is too immodest to suggest that it was not only Harry Gordon who gave *Fittie folk, Kitty folk* its huge local popularity; probably we in STW? played our part too – but the real glory belongs to Archie Hyslop.

27. "Oh Yes We Will. Oh No You Won't."

"I'd like you gentlemen to meet Paul Eliot
of E&B Pantomimes"
— James Donald of HMT, early 1987

A nd we did. And got on famously. He was great company, most amusing, with a fund of show business stories and we were chuffed to be asked by the acknowledged king of pantomime at the time to write a new Scottish pantomime. The background to such a pleasing invitation was that E&B, virtually a pantomime factory, had a production belt of as many as a couple of dozen shows on the go every Christmas in most of the cities and big towns in England, but only the one in Scotland at HMT Aberdeen. This was a challenge; they dearly wanted to break into Glasgow and Edinburgh and saw STW? as a possible means of doing so with a specially written Scottish production which would have at least a three year life-cycle between the only Number One theatres in the country: the King's Glasgow, the King's Edinburgh and HMT Aberdeen.

A good plan, the only drawback being that both of the Kings', owned by the local authorities of Glasgow and Edinburgh respectively, were locked in an arrangement with one of the big theatres in the North-East of England – Sunderland I think it was, Newcastle having been presumably snaffled by E&B already. Well, the upshot was that despite meetings and negotiations attended by representatives of Glasgow and Edinburgh Councils, E&B and STW?, it proved impossible to break the Glasgow-Edinburgh stronghold and E&B remained strongly linked only to Aberdeen.

Meanwhile Buff and I had written the script and Buff the lyrics for our new pantomime, *Rob Roy*, which we visualised being as much for grown-ups as for children. The folder lies in a drawer gathering dust along with the one containing the ill-fated television comedy *The Italians* – projects which both failed to materialise, but were worth the effort if only for the relief of completion, a feeling I sense beginning to come over me as I detect a faint light at the end of the tunnel of this book… a light which not long ago I feared I would never see.

There were incidental pleasures in relation to *Rob Roy,* all to do with the association with Paul Elliot of whose knowledge, enthusiasm and sense of humour I cannot speak too highly. Maybe that's because there was a fair bit of reciprocal hospitality involved in Aberdeen, London[1] and Edinburgh, but I am sure I remained sober enough to appreciate the genuine support and advice of a man at the top of his game for the efforts of us small beer, which he monitored with patience and good nature.

As part of our research into his world of panto he even arranged for us to see E&B's biggest production that year, *Jack and the Beanstalk* starring Russ Abbott at the Hippodrome, Birmingham. And that really was an eye-opener, not so much for the large cast and high production values which were to be expected, but in respect that at the peak of the season there were three performances a day. Panto people really had to work their socks off, a truth which had to be borne in mind when, in compensation for the disappointment of *Rob Roy* not going ahead, STW? were invited to headline in E&B's next panto at HMT.

Well that was not a difficult decision for Buff and George who

---

[1] E&B's offices at the Aldwych, London, have a fascinating provenance for anyone interested in musical theatre. Above an insignificant and rather scruffy doorway hard on to the pavement there is one of these discreet blue plaques commemorating the connection as the home of Ivor Novello who died in 1951. Just as important, there are a few pretty good watering holes handily adjacent.

immediately and courteously said "No thank you". Performance in panto was not for them. I was curious, however, curious to experiment, to try something different knowing that it would all be over within a month, which was the length of HMT's sensibly limited season. The money was not too bad either, so my answer, with the approval of my STW? partners, was "Yes, thank you". Nor did I regret it for all sorts of reasons, the main one however, being the friendship with that great lad George Duffus as mentioned in Chapter 20.

Paul Elliot was most helpful to STW? in another connection, too. The possibility of STW? going abroad was discussed among ourselves from time to time, but we never got round to doing anything about it until the subject came up in Paul's company. It emerged that he had excellent contacts in Ottawa and Toronto which he was happy to pass on, and thus it was in late August 1988 that I embarked solo on what was a part working holiday, mainly to old friends pressing me to visit, but taking in both these cities and useful appointments with the names Paul Elliot had given us. Ted Demietrie, head of programming at Ottawa's National Arts Centre, showed me round and gave advice on the suitability of three theatres in the complex; Ross Petty, Toronto producer, received me most hospitably and gave me pointers as to the right kind of venue there for STW?

These were fertile fields waiting to be cultivated, but when I got home and reported on my Canadian trip at the next STW? partners' meeting there was not enough enthusiasm to take matters further forward. Although, after much discussion, we didn't take a vote (and if we had, I, ever the optimist, would have voted "Yes, let's go for it") the kind of anti-risk majority feeling that could be expected from a group of people in their mid to late fifties naturally prevailed. And that was fine by me, always happy to accept democratic opinion. It would have been different had we been twenty years younger, but working in Scotland in familiar surroundings was probably enough to cope with for four aging thespians pushing towards their bus passes.

28. Neville's Garden Party

"...not your average garden party 'tis true... It may be safe to assume, in fact, that the idea to throw Neville Garden's Party was born towards the end of a reasonable lunch... and on Sunday 1st August 1993 showbiz friends and colleagues of the popular journalist and broadcaster are set for a pretty starry knees-up at the City Halls in Glasgow."
— Ruth Wishart in *The Scotsman*, July 1993

We could not possibly decline an invitation to join this particular party. Neville Garden had been part of our very beginning. For that reason alone we would have gone to support him, but there was more to it than that. When Neville moved from print journalism into broadcasting and became the anchor man on BBC Radio Scotland's early morning show Buff and I were, I think, his very first guests when, as it happened, we were in Edinburgh and opening at the King's for the first time in 1978.

It was a crack of dawn encounter for which our only preparation was a sleep-walk in silence through empty streets from the Caley to the old BBC studios in Queen Street, an eerie place at that time of day. And not a lot better at a civilised hour, I discovered a few years later when I was doing *Naked Radio* from the same location. There could scarcely be a better antidote to weary eeriness, however, than affability, and that was Neville's trademark. He was a model of bonhomie in both his bearded, bespectacled appearance and in his welcome to his studio guests.

Other interviews followed over the years and although these were generally very 'soft', I do recall being embarrassed during a press call on a return visit to the King's when Neville took me aside into some dark corner at the back of the stalls, and out of the blue, or rather out of the usual batch of frothy questions, he said quite sharply, "You must surely be thinking of going full-time, Stephen"…to which I would have said, "Yes" if I had been honest. This was a reply which I could hardly give, however, at a time when I was under all the obligations of my partnership in an Aberdeen law practice, never mind loyalty and priority of disclosure to family and friends.

Thus caught out I waffled and babbled in such a negative and inadequate way that Neville took pity and let me off the hook of further searching questions. He was a real gentleman and having also enjoyed his company socially on one or two occasions, we were sorry to hear that he had been the victim of a BBC re-organisation and change of house style, in consequence of which his services were no longer required. That prompted a sort of mini palace revolution in which the feisty broadcasters Ruth Wishart and Lesley Riddoch, thoughtful and generous ladies as they were at heart, played a leading part and which led to Neville's Garden Party, the purpose of which was to help establish a trust fund for his young family.

Actually the evening was not much of a knees-up, nor was it very starry if you consider those who might have been on the bill but weren't. However, those who were there in noble support provided a jolly good programme, and for the record and in no particular order they were Linda Ormiston,[1] Elaine C. Smith, Pat Kane, Johnny Beattie and three sad old buffers called STW?, introduced by fellow presenters and colleagues of Neville's, including such as John Milne and Colin Bell. And overshadowing all, to open and close the show was the BBC Scottish Symphony Orchestra with the man himself conducting the finale in handsome style.

---

[1] I cannot resist making nice noises about this glorious lady who has become a good pal over the years. George knows her better than I do because he has accompanied her on many occasions, but he's never played golf with her as I have – once. Which was enough – and that's praise because Linda's sense of humour and gift for comedy are more than a match for her operatic talents – which are marvellous. And she can sing a bit, too.

29. A National Trust for Scotland Cruise
or The Scottish Middle-Class At Sea

"The Black Prince is a cruise ship of some 11,210 tons with a passenger capacity of 412 and a crew of 210. Throughout its seven decks the public facilities comprise two traditional dining-rooms, one buffet-style dining-room, a show lounge with bar, a piano lounge with bar, an outdoor pool with whirlpool and a games room"

— Summary on website

The wee liner was all of what the blurb said and therefore well-suited to the sort of passenger attracted by the NTS imprimatur, and that sort of passenger was our sort of audience. Did I hear the whisper "bourgeois" again? This must have been recognised by the top brass of the NTS on the advice of their PR man John Forgie and another senior chap i.e. Cruise Organiser Chris Thornton, with whom we had dinner after they had come to the show one night.

What had been a sounding-out exercise on both sides clearly worked to mutual benefit, because there we were a few months later embarking at Leith on a trip up the Baltic. When I say "we" I mean our wives as well as Buff, George and myself. We had all been enlisted to help in various ways, the girls mostly to hold the hands (sometimes quite literally) of the older and frailer passengers and we lads to join the other members of the entertainments group in providing after-dinner – would you believe? – entertainment. As it turned out, the other members of the entertainments group amounted to a grand total of two, Mary Sandeman and James Nicol, singers of considerable distinction and nice with it – good company, and James played a mean game of table-tennis.

And as if the combined forces of Mary, Jim and STW? were not enough to knock the socks off a boatload of geriatrics (an unfair exaggeration, I admit, because we had no burials at sea – not as far as I recollect although, come to think of it, we did wonder what had happened to the partner of an old chap who took to the dance floor on his own each evening) we had great back-up from John Forgie as a genial and personable master of ceremonies. His great pal, the late John Wilkie, the well-known Edinburgh photographer, was also around to add to the fun, and waiting in the wings to flourish the occasional bit of Scottish colour and noise was Hugh Cheape, piper extraordinaire. Nor was Hugh a lone piper (except, of course, when he was a lone piper). On hand for the special job of piping the passengers aboard and ashore was Jeannie Wheater, wife of Professor Roger Wheater, a senior member of the NTS Council at the time, a little later to become Chairman. As the leaders of the NTS party and the main host and hostess on the cruise, Roger and Jeannie set the tone for the voyage, possessed as they were of boundless charm and friendliness. And energy too – much needed because socialising, their principal function, no matter how enjoyable, can be a most exhausting business.[1]

I speak from experience having socialised quite a bit in my time,

---

[1] I had forgotten, but Eva remembered that there was in fact yet another entertainer on board, independent of the NTS. This was The *Black Prince*'s resident pianist, a most agreeable Filipino gentleman who was rather redundant because of our presence and who was therefore happy to justify himself by staying up late to help entertain the entertainers and any other bibulous insomniacs who chanced along to the piano bar. He tickled the ivories with smooth professionalism for all the standards, but was not so hot on bothy ballads which we tried to teach him during one particularly late session when *The Black Prince* had a Marie Celeste-type funny turn. That's what it spookily felt like when the engines conked out along with most of the lighting, and the ship was totally becalmed in the middle of the Baltic as an enveloping fog rolled in. "What a place to run out of petrol," said Buff.

including that Baltic cruise which took us all the way and many, many gins and tonics up to St. Petersburg and back via such stop-offs as Talinn, Gdansk, Riga and Copenhagen. It was at one of these cities – centres of historic significance each of them, worthy of a long and serious bus tour with translation and many cultural interruptions – that one of the passengers, a former headmistress of quite another era, stern of countenance and disposition, had become mislaid, despite the best shepherding efforts of the NTS staff, including our own ladies.

Let us call the missing grande dame Miss Brodie because, if the famous lady bearing that name had survived into her nineties, this could have been she, independent of mind and spirit as she certainly was, and also of any geographical sense. Which was why, much delayed because of fruitless search and contact with the police, the bus was now returning to the boat one passenger fewer than when it started out at some ungodly hour of the morning. No wonder the old soul had become deranged, wandered off and got lost. To be suddenly, heart-stoppingly, bus-stoppingly found. As the bus screeched to a halt there she was, actually at a bus stop – a municipal bus stop. As she was helped aboard to restrained applause, Miss Brodie was unabashed. "I was not in the least concerned," she declared firmly. "I knew perfectly well that if I waited at a bus-stop my bus would come along eventually."

Bagpipe-playing ladies, foxtrot-dancing solo gentlemen, the Miss Brodies of this world… life's rich tapestry was so well represented on the NTS Cruise that we STW? lot were insipid dullards by comparison. We must have done well enough, however, to be asked back and although Buff declined politely, I returned most enjoyably a couple of times and George became a regular, sometimes with Isabelle as the official medical officer on board, but usually, slightly reluctantly, on his own.

George and his inseparable piano are a joy in their inimitable versatility. But George's problem is his popularity, and the fact that he can never say "No!".

30. Final Fling and the Farewell Tour

"I have just had an idea, folks... how about 'Final Fling'?
— Eva Robertson
after much discussion and many suggestions
on a suitable title for STW?'s last show

Well that was approved pretty quickly – and democratically. The partners' meeting must have taken place about the middle of 1994 by which time, as disclosed in our 1996 blue book, the truth had dawned that we were all pushing sixty – backwards. The hurly-burly of the theatre circuit and the need to change the material for every engagement was getting irksome, so we decided to celebrate our Silver Anniversary, due in September that year, with the announcement of a Farewell Tour. Not so much a tour, perhaps, as a series of visits for a last curtain-call at all the places we had appeared, or as many of them as were prepared to have us back.

Happily most were, and so *Final Fling* and the Farewell Tour took shape, the key booking being His Majesty's, Aberdeen, where we wanted to finish and where to our great satisfaction our last season was also the last booking made before his retiral by Jimmy Donald, the Director who had been such a good friend from the beginning. Everything else then fell gradually into place and so between October 1994 and November 1995 we gallivanted the country visiting old haunts and watering holes and winkling fellow couch-potatoes away from their tellies for a last rendezvous over the footlights with the inhabitants and idiosyncrasies of Auchterturra.

I am in no doubt that Aberdeen University would have qualified both as an old haunt and even more, as a watering hole, but Buckingham Palace was neither. They both, however, shared special places on our itinerary that wonderful year, our Alma Mater near the beginning when, along with Jimmy Donald, we received honorary degrees and[1] Buck House just after the end when we really did meet the Queen to be given MBEs. Although I was mildly disappointed that she didn't mention our chat on the phone twenty years earlier, both were a great thrill and the excuse for a bit of over-indulgence, particularly the latter when we made the trip to London *en masse* and took in several shows.[2]

Our *Final Fling* at HMT lasted four weeks, the curtain finally coming down on Saturday 25th November 1995. That morning the *P&J*, whose goodwill together with that of its sister paper the *Evening Express* we always appreciated, even gave over part of its leader column to us, hitting the nail on the head in a way that touched the heart when it said "…you

---

[1] My Mother was the last of our previous generation to survive (until 2000) and it was particularly pleasing for me that she made it to the graduation. She'd been to the Mitchell Hall about 40 years before, but only at the last gasp (i.e. my last gasp) and not in a wheelchair which she required this time to negotiate stairs and long passages, with the assistance of two stalwart University officers. There's a photograph of her in splendid isolation in the front row before the ceremony began and although she never said, she was always a quiet supporter of STW? and would, I am pretty sure, have been quite proud. I cannot say the same for my dear old Dad who, having died nine years earlier, would have been watching from upstairs in some disbelief, if not disapproval.

[2] One of these was Mack and Mabel in the company of our friends Norrie and Muriel Robertson from Dundee who happened to be in London at the time. When I said to Norrie who "went round" after the show, "Do I take it that you are an angel?" his reply was "No, I'm no' an angel – just maybe a wee cherub". Norrie, a fellow solicitor of long acquaintance and standing, sometime Citizen of the Year of Dundee and a legend in his own teetotal lifetime, was show business daft and generous to a fault; the main fault being that he sometimes managed to persuade the producer of the *Sounds Spectacular* shows at the Whitehall Theatre to allow him on stage to strut his stuff among the chorus girls. "I was terrible," he was the first to admit, "but I just loved it." And the girls loved him.

**Honorary degrees at Aberdeen University in company with Jimmy
Donald and Principal Max Irvine** PHOTO: ABERDEEN JOURNALS

made us laugh at ourselves without making fools of us and that is a rare
and precious gift".

This is a point in the narrative as I am slowly getting round towards
half-thinking of winding down, when the phrase to be most appropriately
used is, "Modesty prevents me…etc…etc". Suffice it to say we could
hardly have been more grateful to receive most magnanimous valedictory
write-ups also by Douglas Kynoch in *The Scotsman* and, a little later, by
Jack Webster in *The Herald*,whose headline ran "Not A Dry Eye In The
House". This referred to the audience on our last night, but could just as
easily have applied to ourselves since the send-off they gave us definitely
came into the category of the North-East highest accolade – "Nae bad at
all".

This did rather delay us from getting cleared up and rid of that damned
make-up for the last time before nipping along to our own party at
Poldino's, the local Italian round the corner. All the usual suspects were
there, a kindness of families and friends not to be repeated until our
Freedom day nearly thirteen years later. These included – and how good
it was of him to come and how right it was for him to be there on our last
night – Neville Garden who had been there on our first night. I think I

Buck House and gongs from the Queen   PHOTO: ABERDEEN JOURNALS

may have got slightly tired and emotional, so not everything is crystal clear in my mind, but I do remember Jimmy Donald calling the company to order in commanding fashion and Jack Webster proposing a most gracious and graceful toast (much as he did at the Freedom Dinner all these years later).

And then Buff, George and I apparently did a Vote of Thanks which I had completely forgotten until, doing a bit of research with the help of Graham and Janet's presentation memento, I discovered a copy of a script which Buff and I had knocked up for the occasion (or it is quite possible that Buff had done it on his own since he's awfully good at that kind of thing). Anyway, I am shameless enough to reproduce it verbatim:

"Ladies and gentlemen – silence please – because –
Buff: We'd like to present Scotland the What?'s answer to the
    BAFTA awards
Steve: Namely the DAFTA awards
George: The Donside and Auchterturra Feel Teuchter
    Awards.
S: These awards are to some wonderful people, without

whom the show would probably have been a lot better.

B: The first category is the award to the best tour organiser and venue explorer. And the nominations for the BEST EXPLORER are –

G: Marco Polo

S: David Livingstone

B: Captain Cook

G: Scott of the Antarctic

S: And McHardy of Gordonians and the Ford Motor Company.

B: And the winner is – John McHardy[3]

G: The next category is for the best SOUND WIZARD and the nominations are -

S: Alexander Graham Bell

G: Signor Marconi – and his partner Mr Cheddar.

B: His partner Cheddar?

S: You've heard of Marconi and Cheese

B: Hideguti Soni of Tokyo

G: And David Eastwood

S: And the winner is – David Eastwood

G: The next category is the best STAGE MANAGER.

B: For those of you who don't know, the stage manager is the all important man in the corner who runs the show.

S: And the nominations for best MAN IN THE CORNER are –

G: Frank Bruno

B: Henry Cooper

S: Muhammed Ali

G: And Peter Garland

---

[3] John McHardy. Known to his wife as 'JAG' (and she to him as 'Bomber Harris', which says far less about a most charming lady than it does about the gung-ho geezer himself) John was our man for organising many one-night engagements on the Rotary Club network. In conducting his recces he explored fearlessly where no show business agent had ever explored before and then signalled us to follow, thus bringing up to scratch our knowledge of the geography of our own country, and allowing us to reach corners untouched by live entertainment since fiery crosses and clan warfare. Like his wanderings, John's enthusiasm knew no bounds and counter-balanced admirably our own idleness.

B: And the winner is Peter Garland[4]

B: The next category is the award for SET DESIGN and its associated skill, painting. And the nominations for best painter are –

S: Leonardo da Vinci

G: Rembrandt

B: Kynoch and Robertson

S: And Edi Swan

G: And the winner is – Edi Swan

S: The next category is the best late night conversationalist

B: The nominations – who are all, strangely enough, also theatre and television directors –

G: Peter Ustinov

S: Clive James

B: Jonathan Miller

G: And Alan Franchi

S: And the winner is – Peter Ustinov

B: Unfortunately Peter can't be with us tonight because he's filming on location in Mintlaw.

G: We were going to have him on video, but arrangements for making the video were cocked up by guess who? – Alan Franchi.

S: We know Alan must be disappointed at not winning the award for best late-night conversationalist.

---

[4] Peter Garland. It was James who persuaded Peter to join us when they got chatting back-stage at the King's, Edinburgh, on one of our early visits there. Not that Peter needed much persuasion – part-time stagehand to stage manager was quite a promotion, although James might have omitted to tell him that all he would be managing on stage was three middle-aged mannies – and that 'stage manager' was just a posh name for doing all sorts of ordinary chores nobody else was keen to do. Anyway it all worked out fine, certainly for us. In between other jobs in a varied career and life-style Peter was always ready to respond to our beck and call. "No problem," was his catch-phrase – no problem getting himself to the most outlandish venue, no problem getting a bare platform all fitted up and functional with only half an hour to spare before the performance, no problem nipping out for a bottle of whisky to fortify the cast, no problem managing to get to our Freedom day in 2008. And for STW? not just "no problem" – to have had Peter's loyalty and friendship over thirty years has been a joy and privilege.

Final Fling after-show party – George, Buff and myself, still taking orders from Jimmy Donald

B: But there is a special award for the longest and latest late-night conversationalist –

G: There are no other nominations. The winner is – Alan Franchi.

B: The next award is a special award in the gift of the Scotland the What? partners.

S: Nae jist a gift – a retiral gift for the lady who handled Warehouse and Dispatch (Records, Tapes and Cassettes) for most of Scotland the What's 26 years.

G: And to present this award, we call upon her head of department all these years.

B: Who, we understand, is a Mr Hunter. Is Mr Hunter here?

S: He's on the telephone.

G: Actually he's spared time between telephone calls to come here tonight and we're most grateful. Come away, Mr Hunter.

B: And the winner of this award for more than 20 years' dedicated and efficient handling of the Scotland the What? cassettes is – Anne Logan.

S: While Mr Hunter is with us, we're going to ask him to make the special award for patience, forbearance and tolerance.

G: The nominations are –

B: Mother Teresa

S: Mary Slessor

G: Florence Nightingale

B: And the woman who for 26 years has put up with Graham's late nights and endless hassle in the service of Scotland the What? – Janet Hunter

S: And the winner is – Janet Hunter.

G: And finally, the last award is the award for BEST BUSINESS MANAGER. The nominations are –

B: The late Robert Maxwell

S: Stewartie Milne

G: Sir Ian Wood

S: Charles Pirie Skene

B: Ebeneezer Scrooge and Graham Hunter

G: And the winner is – Graham Hunter.

Childish eh? But OK I assure you in the context of an undemanding, chattering private party happy to respond even to the high proportion of sausages and knickers of which James Logan himself would have been proud. Luckily for us they were ready to laugh. And what luck for us that people had been ready to laugh for over twenty-six years. What luck for us that another thirteen years down the road on our lovely Freedom day people were still ready to laugh. The inscription on the beautiful silver caskets we received has many fine words, but finishes with "…and, above all, for makin' a'body laugh".

That handshake with which Buff, George and I used to begin every show and with which we finished the last one could not possibly have brought us more luck.

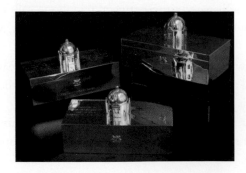